PATTY'S FRIENDS

Patty's Friends

BY

CAROLYN WELLS

AUTHOR OF

TWO LITTLE WOMEN SERIES,
THE MARJORIE SERIES, Etc.

GROSSET & DUNLAP
PUBLISHERS   NEW YORK

CONTENTS

PATTY'S FRIENDS

Patty's Friends

CHAPTER I

AN AFTERNOON TEA

"I WISH I had a twin sister," said Patty; "no, that wouldn't do, either. I wish I were twins, and could be both of them myself."

"What a sensible wish!" commented Nan. "But why do you want to double yourself up in that way?"

"So I could go to two places at once. Here I have two lovely invitations for this afternoon, and I don't know which I want to accept most. One is a musicale at Mrs. Hastings', and the other is a picture exhibition at the New Gallery."

"They sound delightful. Can't you manage to go to both?"

"No, they're too far apart; and they're both at four o'clock, anyway. I think I'll choose the musicale, for I'll surely get another chance to see the pictures."

"Yes, of course you will," agreed Nan, a little absently, for she was reading some newly arrived letters.

The Fairfields were in London, and were comfortably established in the Savoy Hotel. It was April, and though they intended to travel later in the summer, their plans were as yet indefinite, and they were enjoying the many and varied delights of the London season.

To be sure, Nan and Mr. Fairfield were invited to many dinners and elaborate entertainments which Patty was too young to attend, but her time was pleasantly filled with afternoon garden parties or teas, while mornings were often devoted to sight-seeing.

Patty was almost eighteen, and though not allowed quite the untrammelled freedom she would have had in America, she was not kept so utterly secluded as English girls of her age. Sometimes she would go all alone to Westminster Abbey or to the National Gallery, and enjoy hugely a solitary hour or two. At other times, Nan or her father, or some girl friend, would go with her.

The Fairfields had begun their stay in

An Afternoon Tea

London with only a few friends, but these
had introduced others, until now their circle
of acquaintances was large, and the immediate result of this was a sheaf of invitations
in every mail. For, during the season, Londoners are hospitable folk, and give entertainments
morning, noon, and night. At first, the Fairfields
had thought they would take a house, and so
have a home of their own. But Mr. Fairfield
concluded that if Nan had the duties of a housekeeper, her trip would not be a holiday, so he
declared they would live at a large hotel, and
thus have a chance to observe the gay life of
London.

And so cosy and comfortable were their
apartments at the Savoy, that they soon began
to feel quite at home there. And Patty, as we
all know, was one who could adapt herself to
any mode of living.

Of a naturally happy and contented disposition, she accepted everything as it came, and enjoyed everything with the enthusiasm so often
seen in American girls.

It greatly amused her to note the differences
between herself and the English girls.

To her mind, they seemed to have no enthusiasm, no enterprise, and little capacity for enjoy-

ment, while Patty enjoyed every experience
that came to her, whether a visit to Windsor
Castle, a day at Stratford, or a simple afternoon tea in their own rooms.

"I seem to have been set back two or three
years," she said to Nan, one day. "In New
York I was almost a full-fledged young lady, but
over here, I'm treated as a little girl."

"It doesn't matter," said Nan, sensibly.
"You are what you are, and if the different
countries choose to treat you differently, it
doesn't matter, does it?"

"Not a bit. I'm Patty Fairfield, and I'm almost eighteen, whether I'm in California or the
Fiji Islands. But it does amuse me, the way the
Londoners think we live at home. They really
believe American ladies go to market in the
morning, loaded down with diamonds. You
don't often see that in New York, do you,
Nan?"

"No, I don't think I ever saw a New York
matron wearing elaborate jewelry to market.
But then I never go to market myself, and I
don't know many people who do. I think that
bediamonded marketer story is an old tradition,
which is really pretty well worn out."

"And the London ladies needn't talk, anyway. If we did wear jewels to market, it wouldn't be a bit more absurd than the way they dress to go shopping in the morning. Long, trailing, frilly gowns of pink and blue chiffon, with swishing lace-ruffled petticoats, that just drag through the dirt of the streets."

" Now aren't you criticising them as unfairly as they describe us? "

" No, for what I say is true. I've seen them fluttering about. And, anyway, I don't mean to be mean. I like them lots. I just love the London ladies, they're so kind to me, and invite me to such lovely things. Of course I don't care if they choose to wear garden-party clothes along Bond Street. We all have some ridiculous ways."

Pretty Patty was fond of pretty clothes, and the shops of Bond Street held great attractions for her, though she herself wore a real tailor-made costume when shopping. At first, Nan had exercised a supervision over her purchases, but Patty had shown such good taste, and such quick and unerring judgment as to fabrics and colors, that it had come about that Patty more often advised Nan in her choosing, than the other way.

And so, many a pleasant morning was spent

in the beautiful London shops, buying things they wanted, looking at things they did not want, or noting with interest the ways and means peculiar to English shopkeepers.

Thus the days went happily by, and they had already been more than a fortnight in London, while as yet their plans for future travel were unmade. Mr. and Mrs. Fairfield wanted to go to Germany, Switzerland, and other countries, but Patty didn't care so much for that as for English country, or small near-by towns. So the matter was left unsettled, though short and desultory discussions were held now and then.

But oftener their minds were taken up with the doings of the moment, and they complacently left the future to itself.

"Well, then I think I'll go to the musicale," said Patty. "What would you wear?"

"That new light blue chiffon of yours, with the lace bolero is just the thing."

"Yes, and my new broad-leafed chip hat, with the roses piled all over it."

Patty ran away to her own room, and after a time returned in the pretty summer costume.

"How do I look?" she asked, smilingly, of Nan.

An Afternoon Tea

Nan smiled back at the lovely vision, for Patty's vanity was of a mild and innocent sort, and was rather a childish delight in dainty colors and fabrics, than any conceit over her own beauty.

For beautiful Patty certainly was, in a sweet, wholesome, girlish way, and not the least of her charms was her naturalness of manner and her entire lack of self-consciousness.

She looked especially winning in the light, filmy dress, and the big hat, weighed down with roses.

"You look all right, Patty," answered Nan. "That's a duck of a frock, and suits you perfectly. Are you going alone?"

"Yes; father says I may go alone in our own carriage to any afternoon thing. The Hartleys will bring me home, so sha'n't I send the carriage back for you?"

"Yes, I wish you would. I'm going to a tea or two, and then we're dining out. You're to dine with the Hartleys, aren't you?"

"Yes, if it *is* dinner. It's more likely to be schoolroom tea. Mabel Hartley is sixteen, but I doubt if she's allowed at dinner yet."

"Nonsense, of course she is. Well, then, if

[15]

they're sending you home, Louise needn't go after you?"

"No; they'll send somebody. Good-bye, Nan,"

"Good-bye, Patty. Have a lovely time."

"Oh, yes; I always do."

Away went Patty and her frills, and when she reached Chesterton Mansions, she was soon established under the wing of her hostess, Mrs. Hastings.

That lady was very glad to have the pretty American girl as her guest, and she introduced Patty to so many people that it was almost bewildering. But after a time, the music began, and Patty was glad to sit still and listen.

It was very fine music, for that is the sort that Londoners usually offer at their teas, and Patty thoroughly enjoyed the singing and the violin-playing. She was a little afraid that Mrs. Hastings would ask her to sing, but as it was a programme of professionals this did not happen.

When the Hartleys came, Mabel at once made her way to Patty's side and sat down by her.

"I'm so glad to see you again," she said, "and it's so lovely that you're going home with us."

"I'm glad, too," returned Patty, "it was lovely of you to ask me."

An Afternoon Tea

Mabel Hartley was an English girl, and was about as different from Patty as could well be imagined, and perhaps for this reason the two were very good friends. Although they had met only a few times, they liked each other from the beginning, and both were ready to continue the friendship.

Mabel was large and stout, with the solidity which characterises the British young girls. She was large-boned and not very graceful, but she carried herself with a patrician air that told of past generations of good-breeding. Her complexion was of that pure pink and white seen only on English faces, but her pale, sandy hair and light blue eyes failed to add the deeper color that was needed. Her frock was an uninteresting shade of tan, and did not hang evenly, while her hat was one of those tubby affairs little short of ridiculous.

Patty fairly ached to re-clothe her, in some pretty clear color, and a becoming hat.

The girls were politely silent while the music was going on, but in the intervals between the numbers they chattered glibly.

" That's Grace Meredith and her brother Tom just coming in," said Mabel. " I hope they'll come over here; you'll like them, I know."

Patty's Friends

The Merediths did come over, and were promptly introduced to Patty.

"Do you know," said Tom Meredith, as he shook hands in cordial, boyish fashion, "you're the first American girl I've ever met."

"Am I, really?" laughed Patty. "Now don't ask me if we always wear our diamonds to market, for truly the American women who go to market rarely have any diamonds."

"I never believed that diamond story, anyway," responded Tom, gravely, "but I'm glad to have you tell me it isn't true. I'm perfectly unprejudiced about America, though. I'm ready to believe it's the best country in the world, outside of our own little island."

"Good for you!" cried Patty. "Then I'm ready to acknowledge that I like England next best to America."

"Have you been here long?" asked Grace.

"No, only about two weeks, but I love London better every day, and I know I shall love the English country. Just the glimpse I caught coming in the train from Dover was delightful."

"You should see the Hartleys' country place," declared Tom, with enthusiasm. "It's a ripping old house, two hundred years old, and all that. And such parks and orchards! Well!"

An Afternoon Tea

"I hope you will come to see it, Patty," said Mabel, a little wistfully, and Patty wondered why the girl's tone had in it a note of sadness.

But just then, as the music was over, Mrs. Hastings asked them to go to the tea-room, and the group of young people followed in her wake.

"You girls sit here," said Tom, selecting a jolly-looking alcove, with window-seats and red cushions, "while I stalk some food."

He was back in a few moments, followed by a waiter, who brought a tray of teacups and plates of sweet cakes.

Tom, himself, bore triumphantly a covered silver dish.

"Muffins!" he announced, in a jubilant voice. "Hot, buttered muffins! Crickets, what luck!"

The hot muffins, buttered and quartered, were indeed delicious, and England and America seemed at one in showing an appreciative appetite for them.

"We don't have these in America," said Patty, surveying her bit of muffin with admiration. "We have good sandwiches, though."

"We almost never have sandwiches," said Grace.

Patty's Friends

"You don't need to," said Patty, quickly. "Your wonderful bread and butter is too good to be spoiled with a sandwich filling of any sort."

" 'Most all things are good eating at an afternoon tea," observed Tom. " Somehow, at five o'clock I'm always so hungry I could eat a brickbat if it were toasted and buttered."

" Afternoon tea is really an acquired taste with us," said Patty. " You seem to have it naturally, even when you're alone, but we only have it when we have guests."

" Really? " said Mabel, in astonishment. " Why, we'd as soon think of omitting breakfast or dinner as tea."

" It's a lovely meal," said Patty, giving a little sigh of satisfaction, as her last crumb of muffin disappeared. " Such good things to eat, and then it's so cosy and informal to sit around in easy chairs, instead of at a big table."

" But the ideal place for tea is on the lawn," said Tom. " The open air and the trees and birds and flowers are even a better setting for it, than an interior like this."

" I hope I shall have that kind this summer," said Patty. " I'm invited to several country houses, and I know I shall enjoy it immensely."

An Afternoon Tea

"Indeed you will," said Mabel, and again Patty thought she detected a shade of sadness in her friend's eyes.

But if Mabel was not exactly gay, Grace Meredith made up for it. She was full of fun and laughter, and both she and Tom made comical speeches until Patty feared she would disgrace herself laughing.

"What's the joke?" asked Mrs. Hartley, coming to collect her young people and take them home.

"Tom is making verses about the people here," explained Grace. "Tell Mrs. Hartley the one about the violinist, Tom."

"Don't think it's rude, Mrs. Hartley," said young Meredith; "truly, it isn't meant to be. But for that classic-browed genius, with his chrysanthemum of tawny-colored hair, isn't this a pleasant token of regard and esteem?

"This is our latest social lion,
    So, to look modest, he's tryin' and tryin'."

"It's very beautiful," said Mrs. Hartley, smiling, "and I daresay Professor Prendergast would enjoy it himself, were he to hear it."

"He might," said Tom, doubtfully, "but

musicians rarely have a sense of humour, at least, about themselves."

" That's true," agreed Mrs. Hartley, " and now, Mabel and Miss Fairfield, we must be going on."

Good-byes were soon said, and in the Hartleys' carriage Patty was taken away to her first visit in an English home.

CHAPTER II

RIDDLES AND GAMES

MUCH to Patty's satisfaction Mabel Hartley was in the habit of dining with her elders and was not condemned to " schoolroom tea."

The family was not large, consisting only of Mrs. Hartley, her mother, Mrs. Cromarty, her two sons, and Mabel. The sons, Sinclair and Robert, were big, stalwart fellows, a few years older than Mabel.

Patty liked them at once, for they were cordial and hearty in their greetings, and quite at ease in their conversation.

" I say, Mater," began Bob, after they were seated at dinner, " there's a stunning garden-party on at Regent's Park next week. Don't you think we can all go? Tickets only two shillings each."

" What is it, my son? A charity affair? "

" Yes. Rest cure for semi-orphans, or something. But they've all sorts of jolly shows, and the Stagefright Club is going to give a little original play. Oh, say we go!"

"I'll see about it," answered Mrs. Hartley. "Perhaps, if we make up a party, Miss Fairfield will go with us."

"I'd love to," said Patty. "I've never seen a real English garden party."

"Oh, this isn't a real English garden party in the true sense," said Sinclair. "To see that, you must be in the country. But this is a public London garden party and typical of its sort. You'll like it, I'm sure. Will you go with us, Grandy?"

At first it seemed incongruous to Patty to hear the dignified Mrs. Cromarty addressed by such a nickname, but as she came to know her better, the name seemed really appropriate. The lady was of the class known as *grande dame,* and her white hair and delicate, sharply-cut features betokened a high type of English aristocracy. Her voice was very sweet and gentle, and she smiled at her big grandson, as she replied:

"No, my boy; I lost my taste for garden parties some years ago. But it's a fine setting for you young people, and I hope Emmeline will take you all."

"Mother said she'd see about it," said Mabel,

Riddles and Games

"and that's always the same as 'yes.' If it's going to be 'no,' she says, 'I'll think it over.'"

" It's a great thing to understand your mother-tongue so well," said Patty, laughing; "now I shouldn't have known those distinctions."

" We have a wonderful talent for languages," said Sinclair, gravely. " Indeed, we have a language of our own. Shall I teach it to you? "

" You might try," said Patty, " but I'm not at all clever as a linguist."

" You may not learn it easily, but it can be taught in one sentence. It consists in merely using the initial of the word instead of the word itself."

" But so many words begin with the same initial," said Patty, bewildered at the idea.

" Yes, but it's ever so much easier than you'd think. Now listen. Wouldn't you understand me if I said: 'D y w t g t t g p?'"

" Say it again, please, and say it slowly."

Sinclair repeated the letters, and Patty clapped her hands, crying: " Yes, yes, of course I understand. You mean 'Do you want to go to the garden party?' Now, listen to me while I answer: Y I w t g i i d r."

" Good! " exclaimed Mabel. " You said:

' Yes, I want to go, if it doesn't rain.' Oh, you are a quick pupil."

" But those are such easy sentences," said Patty, as she considered the matter.

" That's the point," said Bob, " most sentences, at least, the ones we use most, *are* easy. If I should meet you unexpectedly, and say H d y d? you'd know I meant How do you do? Or if I took leave, and said G b, you'd understand good-bye. Those are the simplest possible examples. Now, on the other hand, if I were to read you a long speech from the morning paper, you'd probably miss many of the long words, but that's the other extreme. We've talked in initials for years, and rarely are we uncertain as to the sense, though we may sometimes skip a word here and there."

" But what good is it? " asked Patty.

" No good at all," admitted Bob; " but it's fun. And after you're used to it, you can talk that way so fast that any one listening couldn't guess what you are saying. Sometimes when we're riding on an omnibus, or anything like that, it's fun to talk initials and mystify the people."

" D y o d t? " said Patty, her eyes twinkling.

" Yes, we often do that," returned Bob, greatly gratified at the rapid progress of the new pupil.

Riddles and Games

"You must be fond of puzzles, to catch this up so quickly."

"I am," said Patty. "I've guessed puzzles ever since I was a little girl. I always solve all I can find in the papers, and sometimes I take prizes for them."

"We do that too," said Mabel; "and sometimes we make puzzles and send them to the papers and they print them. Let's make some for each other this evening."

After dinner the young people gathered round the table in the pleasant library, and were soon busy with paper and pencils. Patty found the Hartleys a match for her in quickness and ingenuity, but she was able to guess as great a proportion of their puzzles as they of hers.

After amusing themselves with square words and double acrostics, they drifted to conundrums, and Bob asked:

"Which letter of the Dutch alphabet spells an English lady of rank?"

"That's not fair," objected Patty, "because I don't know the Dutch alphabet."

"That doesn't matter," said Mabel, "you can guess it just as well without."

"Indeed I can't, and besides I don't know the names of all the English ladies of rank."

"That doesn't matter either," said Sinclair, smiling; "it spells a title, not a name; and one you know very well."

"I can't guess it, anyway," said Patty, after a few moment's thought. "I give it up; tell me."

"Why, Dutch S," said Bob, and Patty agreed that it was a good catch.

"Now, I'll catch you," said Patty. "You all know your London pretty well, I suppose, and are familiar with the places of interest. Well, Mabel, why is your nose like St. Paul's?"

Mabel thought hard, and so did the boys.

"Is my nose like St. Paul's, too?" asked Bob, thoughtfully, stroking his well-shaped feature.

Patty looked at it critically. "Yes," she said, "and so is Sinclair's. But why?"

At last they gave it up, and Patty said, triumphantly, "Because it is made of flesh and blood."

They all screamed with laughter, for they quickly saw the point, and realised that it was the historic character referred to, and not the cathedral.

"Here's one," said Sinclair: "Where did the Prince of Wales go on his eleventh birthday?"

Riddles and Games

But Patty was quite quick enough for this. " Into his twelfth year," she answered promptly. " And now listen to this: A man walking out at night, met a beggar asking alms. The man gave him ten cents. He met another beggar and gave him fifteen cents. What time was it? "

" Time for him to go home," declared Bob, but Patty said that was not the right answer.

" Springtime," guessed Mabel, " because the man was in such a good humor."

" No," said Patty, " it was quarter to two."

Her hearers looked utterly blank at this, and, suddenly realising that they were not very familiar with American coins, Patty explained the joke. They saw it, of course, but seemed to think it not very good, and Sinclair whimsically insisted on calling it, " a shilling to Bob," which he said was equally nonsensical.

" Give us one of your poetry ones, Grandy," said Bob to Mrs. Cromarty, who sat by, quietly enjoying the young people's fun.

" Miss Fairfield may not care for the old-fashioned enigma, but I will offer this one," and in her fine, clear voice the old lady recited her verse with elocutionary effect:

Patty's Friends

" Afloat upon the ocean
    My graceful form you see;
The protector of the people,
    The protector of a tree.
I often save a patient,
    Though a doctor I am not;
My name is very easy,
    Can you tell me, children? What? "

The others had heard this before, and when
Patty promptly guessed " Bark," Mrs. Cromarty was distinctly pleased with her quick-
wittedness.

Then lemonade and wafery little cakes were
brought in, that the puzzlers might refresh
themselves.

The atmosphere of the Hartley household was
very pleasant, and Patty felt much more at
home than she had ever expected to feel among
English people. She made allusion to this, and
Bob said: " Oh, this place isn't homey at all,
compared with our real home. You must come
to see us down in the country, mustn't she,
mother? "

" I should be very glad to welcome you there,
my dear," said Mrs. Hartley, smiling at Patty,
" and I trust it may be arranged. We have

this apartment for only a few weeks longer, and then we shall go back to Leicester."

" I'm in no haste to go," declared Mabel. " I love Cromarty Manor, but I want to stay in London a little longer. But when we do go, Patty, you surely must visit us there."

" Indeed I will, if I can manage it. My parents want me to go with them to Switzerland, but I'd much prefer to spend the summer in England. I have ever so many delightful invitations to country houses, and they seem to me a lot more attractive than travelling about. I suppose I ought to care more about seeing places, but I don't"

" You're quite young enough yet," said Mrs. Hartley, " to look forward to travelling in future years. I think some experiences of English life would be quite as advantageous for you."

" I'll tell father you said that," said Patty. " Then perhaps he'll let me have my own way. But he usually does that, anyway."

" You'd love Cromarty Manor," said Bob, enthusiastically. " It's so beautiful in spring and early summer."

" But not half as grand as other houses where Patty's invited," said Mabel, and again the shadow crossed her face that seemed always to come when she spoke of her country home.

"Grandeur doesn't count in the country," declared Bob. "That belongs to London life. Other places may be larger or in better condition than ours, but they *can't* be more beautiful."

"That is true," said Mrs. Cromarty, in her quiet way, which always seemed to decide a disputed point. And then it was time to go home, and Mrs. Hartley sent Patty away in her carriage, with a maid to accompany her. The woman was middle-aged, with a pleasant voice and a capable manner. She chatted affably with Patty, and dilated a little on the glories of the Cromarty family.

Patty realised at once that she was an old family servant, and had earned a right to a little more freedom of speech than is usual to English domestics.

"Oh, yes, Miss," she said; "it's a wonnerful old place, that it is. And if the dear lady only 'ad the money as is 'ers by right, she'd keep it up lordly, that she would."

Patty wondered what had become of the money in question, but Sarah said no more concerning it, and Patty felt she had no right to ask.

Riddles and Games

" You live with them, then, in the country? "
she said.

" Yes, Miss, I've allus lived with them. My
mother was housekeeper at the Manor when Miss
Emmeline married Mr. 'Artley. Oh, he was the
fine gentleman. Dead now, this ten year come
Whitsuntide. Master Bob, he's the image of
his father. Are you warm enough, Miss? "

Sarah's quick transit from reminiscences to solicitude for her comfort almost startled Patty,
but she was getting used to that peculiarity of
the British mind.

" Yes, thank you," she said, " and anyway,
we're home now. Here's the Savoy."

Mr. Fairfield and Nan had not yet arrived,
so the good Sarah attended Patty to her own
apartment and gave her over to Louise, who
awaited her coming.

Louise helped her off with her pretty frock, and
brought her a beribboned négligée, and Patty
curled up in a big armchair in front of the
fire to think over the evening.

" These wood-fires are lovely," she said to
herself, " and they do have most comfortable
stuffed chairs over here, if they only knew
enough to put rockers under them."

Patty was a comfort-loving creature, and often

[33]

bewailed the absence of the rocking-chairs so dear to her American heart. Soon her parents came in and found her sound asleep in the big chair.

She woke up, as her father kissed her lightly on the forehead.

"Hello, Prince Charming," she said, smiling gaily at the handsome man in evening clothes who stood looking down at her.

"I suppose you want a return compliment about the Sleeping Beauty," he said, "but you won't get it. Too much flattery isn't good for a baby like you, and I shall reserve my pretty speeches for my wife."

"Oh, I'll share them with Patty," laughed Nan, "but with no one else."

"Tell us about your evening, girlie," said her father. "Did you have a good time?"

"Fine," said Patty. "The Hartleys are lovely people; I like them better than any I've met in London, so far. And they do puzzles, and ask riddles, and they're just as clever and quick as Americans. I've heard that English people were heavy and stupid, and they're not, a bit."

"You mustn't believe all you hear. Are they a large family?"

" Not very. Two sons, one daughter, and the mother and grandmother. Mabel's father has been dead for years. And they want me to visit them at their home in Leicester this summer. Can't I go? "

" Desert your own family for foreigners! "

" Yes; I do want to go there and to some other country places while you and Nan go touristing about. Mayn't I? "

" We won't decide now. It's too near midnight for important matters to be discussed. Skip to bed, chickabiddy, and dream of the Stars and Stripes, lest you forget them entirely."

" Never! " cried Patty, striking a dramatic attitude.

" Though English people may be grand,
My heart is in my native land! "

And humming the Star-spangled Banner, she went away to her own room.

CHAPTER III

"I FEEL in a gay mood," said Nan, as she clasped Patty round the waist, and always ready for a dance, Patty fell into step, and the two waltzed round the room, while Patty sang tum-te-tum to the air of a popular song.

"As if you two ever felt any other way!" exclaimed Mr. Fairfield, smiling at them from the depths of his easy chair. "But what does this gay mood betoken? I suppose you want to drag me out to the theatre or opera to-night."

Mr. Fairfield's pleasant smile belied his pretense at sharpness, and he waited to hear a reply.

"That would be lovely," said Nan, "and we'll go if you invite us. But what I had in mind is this: I'd like to dine in the Restaurant."

"Good!" cried Mr. Fairfield. "I feel gay enough for that, myself, and we haven't dined there for nearly a week."

The Fairfields had a complete apartment of

their own, and when not invited out, usually dined quietly in their own dining-room. But occasionally, when the mood took them, they dined in the great Savoy Restaurant, which was a festive pageant indeed.

Patty loved to sit at a table there, and watch the beautiful women in their elaborate gowns, and their handsome, stalwart escorts, who were sometimes in brave uniforms.

The splendid scene would have palled upon them, had they dined there every evening, but as a change from their small family dinner it was delightful.

" We'll wear our dress-up frocks," said Patty, " and perhaps my White Lady will be there again."

" Your White Lady? " asked Nan. " Who is she? "

" That's just what I can't find out, though I've asked several people. But she's the most beautiful lady, with a haughty, proud face, and sad eyes. She always wears white, and there's an elderly lady who is sometimes with her. A strange-looking old lady in black, she is; and her face is like a hawk's."

" Oh, I remember those people; they always sit at the same table."

Patty's Friends

" Yes, I think they live here. But she is so sweet and lovely I'd like to know her. I make up stories about her all to myself. She's like Ginevra or the Lady of Shalott."

" You're too fanciful, Patty. Probably she's the Duchess of Hardscrabble."

" She looks like a Duchess, anyway. And also, she looks like a simple, sweet, lovely lady. I'm going to ask father to find out who she is."

A little later the Fairfields went down to dinner.

Nan wore an exquisite gown of embroidered yellow satin, and Patty wore a frilled white silk muslin. It was a little low at the throat, and was very becoming to her, and in and out of her piled-up curls was twisted a broad white ribbon, which ended in front in a saucy cluster of bows, after the prevailing fashion.

" This is great fun," said Patty, as she took her seat with a little sigh of content. " I just love the lights and flowers and music and noise——"

" Can you distinguish the music from the noise? " asked her father, laughing.

" I can if I try, but I don't care whether I do or not. I love the whole conglomeration of sounds. People laughing and talking, and a sort of undertone of glass and china and waiters."

" That sounds graphic," said Nan, " but the waiters here aren't supposed to make any noise."

" No, I know it, but they're just part of the whole scene, and it's all beautiful together. Oh, there's my White Lady! "

It was indeed a charming young woman who was just entering the room. She was tall and very slender, with a face serene and sweet. Her large, dark eyes had a look of resignation, rather than sadness, but the firm set of her scarlet lips did not betoken an easily-resigned nature.

With her was the elder lady of whom Patty had spoken. She was sharp-featured and looked as if she were sharp-tempered. She wore a rather severe evening gown of black net, and in her gray hair was a quivering black aigrette.

In contrast to this dark figure, the younger lady looked specially fair and sweet. Her trailing gown was of heavy white lace, and round her beautiful throat were two long strings of pearls. She wore no other ornament save for a white flower in her hair, and her shoulders and arms were almost as white as the soft tulle that billowed against them.

Patty's Friends

It chanced that Mr. Fairfield's table was quite near the one usually occupied by these two, and Patty watched the White Lady, without seeming to stare at her.

"Isn't she exquisite?" she said, at last, for they were not within earshot, and Nan agreed that she was.

As the dinner proceeded, Patty glanced often at the lady of her admiration, and after a time was surprised and a little embarrassed to find that the White Lady was glancing at her.

Fearing she had stared more frankly than she realised, Patty refrained from looking at the lady again, and resolutely kept her eyes turned in other directions.

But as if drawn by a magnet, she felt impelled to look at her once more, and giving a quick glance, she saw the White Lady distinctly smiling at her. There was no mistake, it was a kind, amused little smile of a most friendly nature.

Patty was enchanted, and the warm blood rushed to her cheeks as if she had been singled out for a great honour. But frankly, and without embarrassment, she smiled back at the lovely face, and returned the pleased little nod that was then given her.

The White Lady

"Patty, what *are* you doing?" said Nan; "do you see any one you know?"

"No," said Patty, slowly, almost as one in a dream, "my White Lady smiled at me,—that's all,—so I smiled back at her, and then we bowed."

"You mustn't do such things," said Nan, half smiling herself, "she'll think you're a forward American."

"I am an American," replied Patty, "and I'd be sorry to be called backward."

"You never will be," said her father. "Well, I suppose you may smile at her, if she smiles first, but don't begin sending her anonymous notes."

"Nonsense," said Patty, "but you two don't know how lovely she is when she smiles."

Mr. and Mrs. Fairfield were seated with their backs to the lady in question, and could not see her without slightly turning their heads, while Patty, opposite them at the round table, faced her directly.

"You're fortunate in your position," observed her father, "for were you seated here and we there, of course she would have beamed upon us."

"She isn't beaming," cried Patty, almost in

dignantly; " I won't have that angelic smile called a beam. Now, you're not to tease. She's a sweet, dear lady, with some awful tragedy gnawing at her heart."

" Patty, you're growing up romantic! Stop it at once. I'll buy the lady for you, if you want her, but I won't have you indulging in rubbishy romance like that, with nothing to base it on."

Patty looked at her father comically.

" I don't believe you'd better buy her, Daddy, dear," she said. " You know you often say that, with Nan and me on your hands, you have all you can manage. So I'm sure you couldn't add those two to your collection; for I feel certain wherever the White Lady goes the Black Lady goes too."

The subject was lost sight of then, by the greetings of some friends who were passing by the Fairfields on their way out of the Restaurant.

"Why, Mrs. Leigh," exclaimed Nan, " how do you do? Won't you and Mr. Leigh sit down and have coffee with us? Or, better yet, suppose we all go up to our drawing-room and have coffee there."

After Patty had spoken to the newcomers and

The White Lady

was sitting silent while her elders were talking, she looked up in surprise as a waiter approached her. He laid a long-stemmed white rose beside her plate, and said, quietly, "From Lady Hamilton, Miss."

Involuntarily, Patty glanced at the White Lady, and seeing her smile, knew at once that she had sent the rose.

As Patty explained the presence of the flower to the others, Mrs. Leigh glanced across, and said: "Oh, that's Lady Hamilton! Excuse me, I must speak to her just a moment."

"Who is Lady Hamilton?" asked Nan of Mr. Leigh, unable longer to repress her interest.

"One of the best and most beautiful women in London," he replied. "One of the most indifferent, and the most sought after; one of the richest, and the saddest; one of the most popular, and the loneliest."

All this seemed enough to verify Patty's surmises of romance connected with the White Lady, but before she could ask a question, Mrs. Leigh returned, and Lady Hamilton came with her. After introductions and a few words of greeting, Lady Hamilton said to Mr. Fairfield: "I wonder if you couldn't be induced to lend me your daughter for an hour or so. I will do my best to entertain her."

" Indeed, yes, Lady Hamilton; and I think you will find her quite ready to be borrowed. You seemed to cast a magic spell over her, even before she knew your name."

" I must confess that I have been wanting to meet her; I have searched this room in vain for some mutual friend who might introduce us, but until I saw Mrs. Leigh over here, I could find no one. Then, to attract Mrs. Leigh's attention, in hope of her helping me, I sent over a signal of distress."

" I took it as a flag of truce," said Patty, holding up the white rose as it trembled on its stem.

" I thought it was a cipher message," said Nan, smiling. " Patty is so fond of puzzles and secret languages, I wasn't sure but it might mean ' All is discovered; fly at once! ' "

" It means ' all is well '," said Lady Hamilton, in her gracious way; " and now I must fly at once with my spoil."

She took possession of Patty, and with a few words of adieu to the others, led her from the room. The lady in black rose from the table and followed them, and Patty entered the lift, blissfully happy, but a little bewildered.

The White Lady

"We'll have our coffee right here," said Lady Hamilton, as having reached her drawing-room, she proceeded to adjust some dainty gilt cups that stood on a small table. "That is, if you are allowed to have coffee at night. From your roseleaf cheeks, I fancy you drink only honeydew or buttercup tea."

"No, indeed; I'm far too substantial for those things," said Patty, as she dropped into the cosy chair Lady Hamilton had indicated; "and for over a year now, I've been allowed to have after-dinner coffee."

"Dear me! what a grown-up! Miss Fairfield, this is Mrs. Betham, my very good friend, who looks after me when I get frisky and try to scrape acquaintance across a public dining-room."

If Lady Hamilton was lovely when she was silent, she was doubly bewitching when she talked in this gay strain. Little dimples came and went in her cheeks, so quickly that they had scarcely disappeared before they were back again.

Mrs. Betham bowed and spoke politely to Patty, but her voice was quick and sharp, and her manner, though courteous, was not attractive.

"I doubt the coffee's hot," she said, as a waiter, who had just brought it in, was filling the tiny cups.

"It's steaming," said Lady Hamilton, gaily, and Patty saw at once that whatever it was that made her new friend sorrowful, it was not the grumbling tones of Mrs. Betham.

"It's quite too hot, Julia," she went on; "unless you're careful, you'll steam your throat."

"Not I," growled Mrs. Betham. "I'm not such a stupid as that. But I must say I like my coffee at a table like a Christian, and not setting my cup in my lap, or holding it up in the air."

"Dear me, Julia," said Lady Hamilton, with great solicitude expressed on her face; "dear me, your gout must be very bad to-night. It makes you quite cross. Poor dear!"

Mrs. Betham sniffed at this, but a grim smile came into her eyes, and Patty concluded she was not quite so grumpy as she seemed.

After the coffee was finished, and the tray taken away, Mrs. Betham excused herself and went off to her own room.

"The way it began," said Lady Hamilton, as if to explain her interest in Patty, "was one day when I went through the corridors and

The White Lady

passed your drawing-room, and the door was a little mite ajar, and I heard you singing. I am very fond of just that high, sweet kind of voice that you have, and I paused a few moments to listen to you. Then afterward I saw you in the dining-room two or three times at luncheon or dinner, and I took a fancy to know you, for I felt sure I should like you. Do you mind coming to see me once in a while, my dear? I am very lonely."

"Mind! No, indeed!" cried Patty, impetuously throwing her arms around her new friend. "I loved you the first time I ever saw you. But why do you say you are lonely? You, a great lady."

"I will tell you my story in a few words," said Lady Hamilton. "For I suppose you would hear it from others, and I would rather tell it you myself. I am the daughter of Sir Otho Markleham. Of course, if you were a Londoner, you would know all this, but as you're not, I'll tell you. Well, I am Sir Otho's only daughter, and four years ago, when I was just eighteen, I ran away from home and married Lord Cecil Hamilton. He was a good man, but he had quarrelled with my father on a point of politics, and my father disapproved of the match. He disowned me as his daughter, though he said he would always continue the allowance I had had as a girl. I was glad of this, not only because Lord Hamilton, though a man of good fortune, was not a wealthy man, but also because it seemed to show my father had not entirely cast me off. But he forbade us to go to his house, and we went to Paris and lived there for a year. After one year of happy married life Cecil died, and since then my only aim in life has been to be reconciled to my father. But he will not have it, or at least he won't have it unless I make the first overtures toward peace."

"And won't you?" cried Patty, in astonishment.

"Not I! I am not to blame. The two men quarrelled, and now that Cecil is gone, why should my father hold the feud against me? It is not my place to ask his pardon; I've done nothing wrong."

"You ran away from home," said Patty, thinking only of the justice of the case, and quite forgetting that she was seeming to censure a titled English lady.

"Yes, but that was not wrong. Father knew that Cecil was a fine, honourable man, of an old family.' He had no right to forbid my marriage because of a foolish personal disagreement."

" Your mother? " said Patty.

" My mother died when I was a child," said Lady Hamilton, and at once Patty felt a new bond of companionship.

" I lived alone with my father, in our great house in London, and I had a happy and uneventful life, until Cecil came. Since his death, I've longed so to go home to my father, and be at peace with him, but though many kind friends have tried to bring about a reconciliation, they haven't been able to do so."

" And so you live here alone at the Savoy? "

" Yes, with Mrs. Betham, who is really an old dear, though sometimes she grumbles terribly."

" And do you go into society? "

" I've begun to go a little, of late. Cecil made me promise I'd never wear black dresses, so I've worn white only, ever since he died, and I suppose I always shall. That is, in the house. I have black street gowns. But I can't seem to care for gay parties as I used to. I want father, and I want my home."

" Is your father in London? "

"Oh, yes; he's a Member of Parliament. But he's of a stubborn and unyielding nature."

"And so are you?"

"And so am I. Now, let's drop the subject of myself for the present, while you sing for me. Will you?"

"Yes, indeed," said Patty, warmly; "with more pleasure than I ever sang for any one else."

CHAPTER IV

A FLORAL OFFERING

AS the days went by, Patty and Lady Hamilton became close friends. Mr. and Mrs. Fairfield approved of the intimacy, for the elder woman's influence was in every way good for Patty, and in return the girl brought sunshine and happiness into Lady Hamilton's life.

They went together to concerts and picture exhibitions, but Patty could rarely persuade her friend to go to a social affair.

"It's absurd, Lady Hamilton," said Patty, one day, " to shut yourself up as you do! All London wants you, and yet you won't go 'round and play pretty with them."

Ignoring this outburst, Lady Hamilton only smiled, and said: " Do you know, Patty, I think it's time you dropped my formal title, and called me by my first name. I'd love to have you do so."

" I've often wondered what your first name is, but I haven't the slightest idea. Tell me."

"No, guess. What name do you think suits me?"

Patty considered.

"Well," she said, at last, "I think it must be either Ethelfrida or Gwendolyn Gladys."

Lady Hamilton laughed merrily. "Prepare yourself for a sudden shock," she said. "I was named for my grandmother, Catharine."

"Catharine! What an absurd name for you! You're not even a Kate. But you *are* Lady Kitty, and I'll call you that, if I may."

"Indeed you may. Father used to call me Kitty, when I was a child, but as I grew older, I preferred my full name."

"Lady Kitty is just right for you, and when you're in the mood you're a saucy puss. Now, listen, the reason for my invasion of your premises this morning is that I want you to go with me this afternoon to a tea on the Terrace of Parliament House."

Patty's tones were very persuasive, and she looked so daintily attractive in her fresh morning gown that few could have refused any request she might make.

Lady Hamilton in a soft, frilly white négligée, was sipping her coffee and looking over her letters when Patty had interrupted the process.

A Floral Offering

She looked at her eager young guest with a slow, provoking smile, and said only:

" Nixy."

" But why not? " said Patty, smiling too, for she knew the Englishwoman had learned the slangy word from herself. " You'd have a lovely time. It's so beautiful there, and the people are always so cordial and pleasant."

" But I don't want to go."

" But you *ought* to want to. You're too young to give up the pomps and vanities of this world. How can I *make* you go? "

" You can't."

" I know it! That's just the trouble with you. I never saw such a stubborn, self-willed, determined——"

" Pigheaded? "

" Yes! and stupidly obstinate thing as you are! So, there now! "

They both laughed, and then Lady Hamilton said more seriously, " Shall I tell you why I won't go? "

" Yes, do, if you know, yourself."

" I know perfectly. I won't go to the Terrace because I'm afraid I'll meet my father there."

" For goodness' sake! Is that the real reason? But you *want* to be reconciled to him! "

"Yes, but you don't understand. We couldn't have a 'Come home and all will be forgiven' scene on the Terrace, in sight of hundreds of people, so if I did see him, I should have to bow slightly, or cut him dead; it would depend on his attitude toward me which I did. *Then* the episode would merely serve to widen the breach, and it would break me up for days."

"I can't understand such conditions," said Patty, earnestly. "Why, if I were at odds with my father, and I can't even imagine such a thing, I'd rush at him and fling myself into his arms and stay there till everything was all right."

"That's just because you're of a different temperament, and so is your father. My father is an austere, unbending man, and if I were on the Terrace and were to fling myself into his arms, he'd very likely fling me into the Thames."

"You'd probably be rescued," said Patty, gravely; "there's always so much traffic."

"Yes, but father wouldn't jump in to rescue me, so I'd only spoil my gown for nothing. Give it up, dear, it's a case outside your experience. Father and I are both too proud to make the first advance, and yet I really believe he wants me as much as I want him. He must be

A Floral Offering

very lonely in the great house, with only the servants to look after him."

" Perhaps he'll marry again," said Patty, thoughtfully; " my father did."

" I wish he would, but I've no hope of that. Now, never mind about my troubles, tell me of your own. Who's taking you to the tea? "

" Mrs. Hastings. But she isn't giving it. We're to sit at some Member's table; I don't know whose. The Merediths will be there, too. Tom and Grace, you know. I like them very much."

" Yes, they're nice children. I know them slightly. Patty, some day I'll give a party for you, here in my rooms. How would you like that? "

" Oh, Lady Kitty, I'd love it! You'd have to come to that, wouldn't you? "

" Yes, indeed, you couldn't drive me away. Let's have a children's party. All dress as children, I mean; little children, or babies."

" Just the thing! I always wanted to see a party like that. I've only heard of them. Can we have it soon? "

" Next week, I think. I'll consult Mrs. Betham, and I think I can coax her 'round to it; though she's bound to wet-blanket it at first."

Patty's Friends

"Oh, yes, you can coax her, I know. How good you are to me! I do have beautiful times. Really too many for one girl. Honestly, Lady Kitty, do you think it's right for me to lead such a butterfly life? I just fly about from one entertainment to another; and even if I'm at home, or alone, I always have a good time. Sometimes I think I'm a very useless member of this busy world."

Lady Hamilton smiled kindly. "How old are you?" she said.

"I'll be eighteen next month."

"And you haven't set the Thames on fire, or won the Victoria Cross yet? But you're just at the age when your type of happy girlhood is often beset with over-conscientious scruples. Don't give way to them, Patty. It is not your lot to do definite, physical good to suffering humanity, like a Red Cross nurse, or the Salvation Army. Nor is it necessary that you should work to earn your bread, like a teacher or a stenographer. But it is your duty, or rather your privilege, to shed sunshine wherever you go. I think I've never known any one with such a talent for spontaneous and unconscious giving-out of happiness. It is involuntary, which is its chiefest charm, but whoever is with you for a

A Floral Offering

time is cheered and comforted just by the influence of your own gladness. This is honest talk, my child, and I want you to take it as I mean it. Don't *try* to do this thing, that would spoil it all; but just remember that you *do* do it, and let that satisfy your desire to be a useful member of this busy world."

"You're such a dear," said Patty, as she caressed her friend's hand affectionately; " if that's all true, and of course it is, since you say so, I'm very glad. But can't I do something more definite, more voluntary? "

" Of course there are always opportunities for doing good,—organised charities and those things that everybody takes part in. But if you want to widen your own field of benefaction, simply know more people. Whether you know them socially or as casual acquaintances, you will almost invariably add happiness to their lives, though it be in the merest trifles. Now, I'm assuming that you have sense enough not to overdo this thing, and thrust yourself upon people who don't want you."

"Madam," said Patty, in mock indignation, "you may trust me. I am an American! "

" You are indeed; and you have what is known

as Yankee good sense, if you are a mere infant."

" Eighteen is pretty old, *I* think; and you're not so very ancient, yourself," retorted Patty; " but I'm willing to sit at your feet and acquire wisdom."

When dressed to go out that afternoon, Patty stopped at Lady Hamilton's door to say good-bye.

" Come in, and let me see if you'll pass muster. Yes, that frilly, flowered muslin is just right for the Terrace; and that hat with long streamers is truly pastoral."

" What's pastoral about the Terrace, pray? "

" Nothing but the ladies' clothes, and the lamb-like demeanour of the M.P.'s."

" I may see your father there."

" You may. But he'll be an exception to the lamb-like ones. Here, let me put these valley lilies in your belt. They rather suit your costume."

" Oh, thank you; they're beautiful. If I see your father, I'll give him a spray and say you sent it."

" Very well; he'll then pitch you and the flow-ers all in the Thames together."

[58]

A Floral Offering

" Well, at least we'll cause a sensation among the lambs. Good-by, Kitty lady."

" Good-bye, little one. Have a good time, and come in to tell me about it when you return."

The tea on the Terrace was a new delight. Patty had been through the Houses of Parliament before, but this was her first experience of that unique function known as the Terrace Tea.

The broad, beautiful space was crowded with tables, and the tables were crowded with people. Merry, chatting, laughing Londoners, Americans, and foreigners mingled in groups and drank tea together.

Mrs. Hastings and Patty were met by their host, Mr. Pauncefote, and escorted to a table, already surrounded by several people.

Patty felt greatly pleased when she found herself seated between Grace and Tom Meredith, and listened with interest as they designated various celebrated people who were strolling by.

" But, after all," she said, at last, " Dukes and Duchesses don't look very different from ordinary people."

" Of course they don't. Why should they? They aren't any different," said Tom. " Indeed, Miss Fairfield, I've vanity enough to believe you'd find me more interesting than some of the Dukes."

" I'm sure you are," laughed Patty, " but if I were introduced to a real Duke, I'd be so scared I wouldn't know what to say."

" Now I call that too bad," declared Tom, with an aggrieved look. " And, pray, why aren't you scared when in my august society? "

" I am," said Patty, dimpling, as she smiled at him, " only I'm successfully striving not to show my quaking fright."

" That's better. I hope the longer you know me, the more awed you'll be of my,—of my——"

" Of your what? " calmly inquired his sister.

" 'Pon my word, I don't know," confessed Tom, good-naturedly; " of my awesomeness, I suppose."

" How do you like London? " said a loud voice, in the tones that are sometimes called stentorian, and Patty suddenly realised that her host was addressing her.

A bit embarrassed at finding the eyes of all at the table upon her, she answered, shyly: " I love it; it is so—so kind to me."

" Bravo! Pretty good for an American," shouted Mr. Pauncefote, who seemed unable to moderate his voice. "And which do you like best, the people or the show-places?"

"The people," said Patty, her embarrassment lost sight of in a flash of mischief. "I like the Members of Parliament better than Parliament House."

"Good! Good!" cried the portly M.P., striking the table with his fist until the cups rattled; "that's true Yankee cleverness. You're a good sort, my child. Are they all like you in America?"

"Yes, I think so," said Patty, demurely; "are they all like you in England?"

Patty's innocent air of inquiry robbed the speech of all effect of pertness, and the genial Mr. Pauncefote roared with delight.

"Ha, ha!" he cried; "all like me in England? No, my child, no! Heaven be praised, there are very few after my pattern."

"That's too bad," said Patty. "I think your pattern is a good one."

"It is," said Tom Meredith. "If we had more statesmen after Mr. Pauncefote's pattern, the House of Commons would be better off."

This speech called forth applause from the other guests, and the host said, loudly: "Pshaw, pshaw!" but he looked greatly pleased.

Patty's Friends

When the tea was over and the party rose from the table, Mr. Pauncefote detained Patty for a moment's chat, while the others broke up into smaller groups or wandered away.

"I want you to meet my daughter," he was saying; "the young lady in gray over there talking to Sir Otho.

"Sir Otho who?" said Patty, quickly, forgetting to respond in regard to Miss Pauncefote.

"Sir Otho Markleham; see the large gentleman with gold-rimmed glasses. She is my youngest daughter, and I know she'd be glad to meet you."

"I'd be delighted," said Patty, but her attention centred on Sir Otho.

Could it be that was Lady Hamilton's severe father? He did not look so obstinate as she had imagined him, but as she drew nearer, she observed the firm set of his square jaw and reversed her opinion.

Sir Otho was very tall and big, and his smoothly brushed hair was light brown without a trace of gray.

He wore closely-trimmed whiskers, of the style known as "mutton-chop," and his cold gray eyes almost glittered as he looked through his glasses. The introduction to Miss Pauncefote

A Floral Offering

implied also an introduction to Sir Otho, and in a moment Patty found herself chatting in a group of which Lady Kitty's father was one.

There was something about the big man that awed her, and she naturally fell into conversation with Miss Pauncefote, while the two gentlemen talked together. But as they were all about to separate, and even after Sir Otho had said good-afternoon, Patty hesitated irresolutely for a second, and then turned back toward him again.

" Sir Otho," she said, timidly.

"Well, ma'am, what is it ? " was the response as he turned in surprise to look at her.

" I am very glad to meet you," said Patty, and as soon as the words were uttered, she realised how absurd they were.

" Thank you, ma'am," said the puzzled gentleman. He was very unresponsive, and showed in his face that he thought little of this exhibition of American forwardness.

" Especially so," Patty went on, " because I know your daughter, Lady Hamilton."

" Bless my soul! " ejaculated Sir Otho Markleham, the red blood dyeing his large face crimson, and his eyes fairly snapping with anger.

" Yes, I do," went on Patty, resolved now to

plunge in desperately, " and she sent you these flowers."

Patty had previously detached two or three of the prettiest sprays of the lilies of the valley, and now held them out, with the air of one fulfilling a trust.

For a moment Sir Otho Markleham looked as if he would really like to pitch the American girl and her flowers into the river, and then, almost mechanically, he took the blossoms from Patty's hand.

Then, with a straight, cold stare at her, he said, in a hard voice: " I have no daughter," and after a stiff, formal bow, he walked away.

CHAPTER V

MISS YANKEE DOODLE

"YOU didn't, really!" exclaimed Lady Hamilton, as Patty gleefully described giving the flowers to Sir Otho Markleham.

"But I did, Kitty, and truly, he *was* mad enough to pitch me into that yellow muddy old river. I greatly admire his self-control in not really doing it. But what eyes he has! So gray and steely, they cut right through me! And he just said, tragically, 'I have no daughter,' and stalked away. But—and this is the main thing—he kept the flowers!"

"How do you know?"

"I watched him. I fully expected he'd fling them straight over Parliament House, but he didn't. He didn't even throw them on the stone floor of the Terrace, and gr-r-rind them 'neath his iron heel! I can't say that he put them in his button-hole, for his back was toward me, but I *know* he kept them."

"Oh, Patty, you are a silly! You think you've

[65]

gone far toward healing the family feud of the Marklehams. But you haven't. My father gave the whole episode no thought at all, unless it was to think of you as an impertinent child."

"Well, it was a wedge," said Patty, doggedly, "and if I ever get another chance at him, I'll hammer it in."

"No, don't, Patty dear; you mean well, I know, but you don't know father's disposition. If he thought you were an intermediary, he'd be more stubborn than ever."

"Huh!" said Patty, more expressively than politely; "I'm not going to make any trouble. Trust your Aunt Patty for that!"

Lady Hamilton laughed, as she always did at Patty's funny American phrases, and the subject of Sir Otho was dropped.

"Better not mix yourself up in other people's quarrels," said Mr. Fairfield, when Patty told him about it. "Your motive is a good one, but an Englishman is not apt to brook interference from an outsider, especially an American."

"Oh, pshaw, Fred; Patty won't do any harm," said Nan. "Patty's tact is a match for any English temper, and if she could bring about a reconciliation, I'd be so glad for that sweet Lady Hamilton."

"All right; I give in. When you two are against me, I hold up my hands."

"We're not against you, Daddy," said Patty, smiling fondly at her father. "You're on our side, only you don't quite realise it."

"I told you she had tact," laughed Nan, "and she grows cleverer every day; don't you, Step-daughter?"

"Yes, Stepmother," replied Patty, gazing at Nan in mock adoration; "since I have you for a model, how could I do otherwise?"

"You're a pair of sillies," said Mr. Fairfield, laughing at their nonsense, "and in a vain endeavour to improve your minds, I think I'll read aloud to you."

"Oh, goody!" cried Patty, for they both loved to hear Mr. Fairfield read. "And mayn't I ask Lady Kitty to come in? She'll sit still as a mouse, I know."

"Certainly, my child; ask any one you like. If you see any people in the corridors, bring them back with you. Perhaps the elevator man will come."

"'Deed he won't be asked," said Patty, indignantly. "I just want my sweet, lovely Lady Kitty."

The sweet, lovely lady was pleased to come,

and did indeed sit still as a mouse, listening to Mr. Fairfield's fine reading.

Then Patty sang one or two of her newest songs, and then Nan declared they must all go down to the Grill Room for a Welsh Rabbit.

This plan enchanted Patty, and after a moment's hesitation, Lady Hamilton agreed. So the evening proved a merry little festivity, and Patty went to bed healthily tired, but healthily happy.

Bob Hartley did not forget his promise to ask Patty to the Garden Party at Regent's Park, and Patty gladly accepted the invitation.

" The only thing that bothers me," she said to Nan, " is that the Hartleys don't seem to have much money, and at a Charity Garden Party there are so many ways to spend, that I fear I'll be a burden to them. It makes me awfully uncomfortable, and yet I can't offer to pay for myself. And with those young men present, I can't offer to pay for the whole party."

" No," agreed Nan. " But you might do something yourself. Invite them all to be your guests at some especial side-show, or booth. There are often such opportunities."

" I hope there will be. The Hartleys are a funny kind of poor. They have a good apart-

ment in London, and their country place is fine.
They have old servants, and keep a carriage,
and all that, and yet they never seem to have
spending money."

" English people are often like that. The keeping up of an establishment comes first with them,
and little personal comforts afterward."

" That isn't my idea of economy," said Patty,
decidedly; " I'd rather spend all I want on flowers and books and pretty hats, and go without
a butler and a footman and even a team of
horses."

" You can't judge, because you've always had
whatever you want."

" Of course; because father is indulgent and
has plenty of money. But if he hadn't, I'd be
just as happy, living in a plainer way."

" Yes, Patty, I believe you would," and Nan
looked at the girl affectionately. " Well, do
your best to help the Hartleys financially this
afternoon without offending them."

" Ah, that's just the trouble. They're so
dreadfully proud they won't accept so much as
a glass of lemonade from one who is their
guest."

" Try it, and see. It may not be so difficult
as you think."

Patty's Friends

So Patty went gaily off to the Garden Party. Mrs. Hartley called for her in her carriage. Mabel was with her, and they were to meet the boys at the park.

It was a beautiful drive, in the open victoria, along the busy streets of the city, and then on out to the green slopes of Regent's Park.

The portion of the park devoted to the Garden Party was gay with booths and flower-stands, tents and arbours, and catch-penny shows of all sorts.

Sinclair and Robert were awaiting them, and also another young Englishman, whom Bob introduced as Mr. Lawton. The latter was a typical Briton, with a slight drawl, and a queer-looking monocle in his right eye.

"Awfully jolly to meet you," he exclaimed, as he shook Mrs. Hartley's hand, and bowed formally to the girls.

He fascinated Patty, he was so exactly like the young Englishmen pictured in *Punch,* and she waited to hear him say "Bah Jove!" But he didn't say it, he contented himself with "My word!" by way of expletive, and though it didn't seem to mean anything, it was apparently useful to him.

"You must jolly well let me be your guide,"

he declared; "Mrs. Hartley and I will lead and the rest of you will follow wherever we go. First, we make the grand tour."

This meant joining a long procession that were sauntering along a board walk, on either side of which were settees filled with people.

Patty, with Sinclair, followed the leaders, and Mabel and Bob followed them.

But their progress was slow, for continually some of the party recognised friends seated alongside, and stopped to speak to them. Patty was introduced so often that she became bewildered, and soon stopped trying to remember who was who.

"You're getting jolly well fagged," said Mr. Lawton, suddenly noticing her expression. "Now, we'll stop this merry-go-round and adjourn to the tea tent."

This they did, and were soon comfortably seated round a tea table.

"Great show, isn't it?" said Bob, enthusiastically. "And you haven't seen half of it yet. There's fortune-telling, and Punch and Judy, and the hat-trimming contest, and I don't know what beside."

Sinclair adroitly paid the tea bill, before Mr. Lawton could do so, though the latter tried.

"Never mind, old fellow," he cried, "I'll get even with you! I hereby invite you all to supper at six o'clock."

"We're pleased to accept," said Patty, promptly; "and I hereby invite you all to the play, or whatever it is, given by the Stagefright Club. I think that's such a lovely name for a dramatic club. Can't we go at once?"

Mrs. Hartley looked a little disturbed at Patty's invitation, but did not demur, and tea being over, they all went toward the tent where the play was to be given. Patty managed to walk ahead with Mr. Lawton, this time, and when they reached the big tent, she offered him her little gold chain-purse, saying, quietly, "Won't you see to the tickets, please?"

"Trust me," said Mr. Lawton, and taking Patty's purse, he bought seats for them all. It was gracefully done, and they all went in in gay spirits and without a trace of embarrassment, thanks to Patty's tact.

The play was very funny. Though only a trifling farce, it was written by professionals, for the benefit of the charity, and was played by the clever amateurs who had chosen such an odd name for their club. The situations in the play were screamingly funny, and Patty shook with

Miss Yankee Doodle

laughter as she listened to the jokes and the merry by-play.

" Hist, she comes! " declared a weird figure in a sepulchral voice, as he waited in the middle of the stage.

" Hist, she comes! "

But nobody came.

" That's her cue," he muttered; " what can be the matter? I say," he cleared his throat and spoke louder: " Hist, she comes! " As the expected entrance was still delayed, he only said: " Well, she ought to be hissed when she does come! " And calmly sat down to wait for her, amid the applause of the audience.

The short playlet soon came to an end, and still shaking with laughter, the party went out again into the beautiful atmosphere which is found on a spring day in Regent's Park.

" Now, my children," said Mrs. Hartley, " I simply cannot walk about any more. I'm going to sit in one of those chairs yonder, for I see some people I know over there. You can amuse yourseves with Punch and Judy, or Ring Toss or whatever you like, and come back to me in an hour or so. Sinclair, look after the little ones, won't you? "

It was a great joke that Sinclair, the oldest

Hartley boy, should look after the others. He had reached the age of twenty, and was much more grave and dignified than Bob and Grace. Mrs. Hartley often declared she could even trust him to match samples for her, so careful was he. So the young people wandered away and spent a delightful hour looking at the beautiful or grotesque sights that adorned the fair.

Patty could not do much financially, but under cover of giving to charity, she bought pretty souvenirs for Mabel and Mrs. Hartley, and laughingly invited the group to be photographed by a Camera Fiend.

This personage was clothed in red, and with black horns and Mephistophelean countenance was made to look as much like a fiend as possible. With outlandish hoots and yells, he posed the group and took several snapshots, which they were to call for later.

As they concluded it was nearly time to drift back to Mrs. Hartley, Patty noticed a gentleman who stood at a little distance, looking at her intently.

"Who's your friend, Patty?" asked Mabel. "Do you know him?"

"Yes," said Patty, slowly. "He's Sir Otho Markleham."

Miss Yankee Doodle

"So he is," said Bob. "I've seen him often, but I don't know him personally."

Sir Otho, still looking at Patty, took a few steps toward her, and then paused irresolutely.

"Please excuse me," said Patty to the others, "I think I'll go speak to him for a minute."

"Do," said Mr. Lawton; "we'll wait for you right here."

Following an impulse, Patty walked directly toward Sir Otho, who looked as if he would like to run away.

"How do you do?" she said, pleasantly, as they met.

"Quite well," he said, but there was no responsiveness in his manner. "Do you wish to speak to me?"

Now after he had first advanced toward Patty, this was a strange question, but she bravely took up the burden of conversation.

"Well, yes," she said, smiling at him prettily; "I want to ask you how you are enjoying the Garden Party."

"I never enjoy anything," he returned, but his face was sad now, rather than angry.

"Oh, what a pity!" said Patty, involuntarily, "and you have such powers of enjoyment, too."

"How do you know that, Miss Yankee Doodle?"

Patty didn't altogether like the name, or rather the tone in which it was said, but she was determined not to get piqued. So she said:

"Oh, because you're such a big, healthy, hearty-looking man; you ought to laugh most of the time."

"Ought I, indeed? But you see I never have anything to laugh at."

At this Patty laughed outright.

"Why, the world is full of things to laugh at, —and you're not blind."

"No, but I don't feel like laughing."

"Don't you ever even feel like smiling?"

"Not often."

"Didn't you feel like smiling just a little bit of a happy smile, when I gave you those flowers the other day? Those flowers—from Kitty."

Sir Otho's face grew dark.

"How dare you mention her name to me?" he cried. "You are a saucy minx! Go away!"

"I won't be sent away like that," declared Patty, looking haughty now. "I'm no child to be scolded for nothing. How dare you speak to me like that? What do you think I am?"

Sir Otho turned red with rage. He choked

Miss Yankee Doodle

and stammered and looked like a choleric old gentleman, as indeed he was.

" I think you're an impertinent Yankee. What do you think I am ? "

Patty looked him squarely in the eye. Her chance had come, and she did not flinch.

" I think," she said, looking steadfastly at him, " I think you're an obstinate, stubborn, selfish, cruel old—Pighead! "

She confessed, afterward, that at that moment she fully expected the irate old man to strike her. But he did not. Instead, he looked at her just a moment in amazement, and then burst into peals of laughter.

Surprised beyond measure, but unable to resist the infectious merriment, Patty laughed too.

" Oh, Miss Yankee Doodle," said Sir Otho, wiping his eyes, " you are most astonishing. The strange part is, you are quite right. I *am* a stubborn old Pighead, but how did you know it? Do I wear my heart on my sleeve to that extent? "

" Have you a heart? " asked Patty, so gravely that Sir Otho again roared with laughter.

" And yet," said Patty, thoughtfully, seeing that frankness pleased the old man, " and yet, no one with such a sense of humour as you seem to have can be wholly bad."

" Oh, thank you! So I'm not wholly bad? Well, that's a comfort; I always thought I was. But your friends are looking this way. I think they want you to rejoin them."

" In a moment," said Patty. " Sir Otho,— won't you—please—send a flower back to my friend, Lady Hamilton? "

" I would do much for any friend of yours," said the strange old man, very gravely, and taking a few steps to a near-by flower stand, he bought a bunch of sweet peas, and said, carelessly, " Give her those, if you like."

Then formally escorting Patty back to her friends, he raised his hat, and walked quickly away.

CHAPTER VI

HERENDEN HALL

"THERE, Kitty lady," said Patty, as she reached the Savoy on her return from the Garden Party, "there's a nosegay from your affectionate father."

Lady Hamilton stared at the bunch of sweet peas that Patty held out to her.

"My word!" she exclaimed, "you are the most amazing child! I suppose he sent them to me just about as much as I sent him those valley lilies you took to him the other day."

Lady Kitty guessed so near the truth that Patty felt a little crestfallen.

"It was more than that," she said. "I asked him to send some flowers to you, and he bought these purposely."

"Did he select sweet peas, himself?"

"Yes."

"That means something, then, Patty dear; for father well knows my fondness for these flowers. Well, you're a dear, good little girl to try to heal the breach, but I can't feel much encouragement. Father is too old and too obstinate ever to forgive me.

"And you're too young and too obstinate to go and beg his forgiveness!"

"Indeed I am! Fancy my meekly returning, like a prodigal daughter, when I haven't done anything wrong!"

"You don't deserve a reconciliation," cried Patty; "you're a hard-hearted little thing,— for all you look so soft and amiable."

"Yes," said Lady Kitty, demurely; "I inherited my father's disposition."

"Indeed, you did; and you'll grow more like him every day you live, if you don't try to be more forgiving."

"I believe you're right, Patty; and perhaps some day I will try. But now let me tell you what's been happening. While you were away, I had a call from that very charming stepmother of yours. And this was the burden of her visit. It seems that she and your father are invited to spend the week-end at a country house, and the question was, where to pack you away for safe-keeping while they're gone."

"And they're going to let me stay with you!" exclaimed Patty, clasping her hands and assuming an ecstatically happy expression.

Herenden Hall

"Well, Mrs. Nan seemed to think that I could keep you in order, though I'm not so sure of it myself. But the strange part is, I also am invited for this same week-end to a most delightful country house, and I have already accepted."

Patty's face fell.

"What is to become of poor little me?" she said. "I don't want to stay with Mrs. Betham."

"No; I've a plan for you. And it's this. I want to take you with me to Herenden Hall, where I'm going, and,—Mrs. Nan says I may."

"Oh, Kitty! You duck! How perfectly lovely!" Patty flew at her friend, and nearly strangled her in a spasmodic embrace.

"You see," went on Lady Hamilton, when she had regained her breath, "I'm so well acquainted with the Herendens, that I can ask an invitation for you; and though you're not really 'out' yet, it will give you a glimpse of the nicest kind of English country-house life."

"It's great!" declared Patty. "I'm wild with excitement. But I care more about being with you than I do about the house-party."

"You won't when you get there. They're really charming people, and the Hall is one of the finest old estates in England."

Patty's Friends

" Shall I have to have some new frocks? "

" We'll look over your wardrobe, and see. I fancy the ones you already have will do. You know you'll be looked upon as scarcely more than a schoolgirl, and you must wear simple, frilly muslins and broad-leafed hats."

" I can even live through that! I don't care what I wear if I'm with you. Three whole days! Will it be three days, Kitty? "

" Three days or more. If they politely ask us to remain a day or two longer we might do so. They're old friends of mine, do you see? And I haven't been there for years, so they'll be glad to see us."

" To see you, you mean. They don't know me, so how can they be glad to see me? "

" Oh, you must,—what is your idiotic American phrase? You must ' make good '! "

" I will," said Patty, laughing to hear the phrase from an Englishwoman, and then she ran away to her own apartment, to talk over affairs with Nan.

" It's a great piece of good fortune," said Nan, " that you're such good friends with Lady Hamilton, for Fred and I couldn't take you with us, and what would have become of you? "

" Oh, I always land on my feet," returned

Herenden Hall

Patty, " I must have been born under a lucky star."

" I believe you were, Pattykins."

" And won't I have the time of my life at Herenden Hall——"

" Oh, Patty, Patty, you must stop using slang. They'll never ask you to Herenden Hall again if you behave like a wild Indian."

" But you see, Stepmother, they look upon me as an infant anyhow, so I may as well have some fun."

" But don't be a hoyden, and do remember that American slang isn't admired over here."

" Yas'm; I'll be good. And I'll say ' Really? ' and ' Only fancy! ' till they'll think I'm the daughter of a hundred Earls."

" I'm not at all worried about your manners," said Nan, serenely. " You usually behave pretty well, but you will talk American instead of English."

" Well, I'll try to make myself understood, at all events. And you're going to have a lovely time, too, aren't you? Isn't it fun! I do like to have all my friends as happy as I am. I suppose you and father will be like two young turtle-doves off on your honeymoon trip."

" Oh, we're always that, even when there's a

great, big girl like you around to make us seem old."

"Well, if you behave as well as you look, I won't be ashamed of you." Patty gazed critically at Nan, and then added, "Though your nose does seem to turn up more than it used to."

Whereupon Nan threw a sofa-pillow at her, which Patty caught and stuffed behind her own curly head.

The Saturday of their departure was a beautiful, bright day, and it was about noon when Patty and Lady Hamilton, accompanied by the latter's maid, took the train from Victoria Station.

It was a long ride to their destination in Kent, and not an especially interesting one, but Patty, in the companionship of her dear friend, was entirely happy. They chatted gaily as the train rolled from one English town to another. At Robertsbridge they had to change to a funny little railroad, which had the strangest cars Patty had ever seen.

They were almost like freight cars, with benches along the sides. There were no tickets, and presently the guard came in to collect their fares, as if in a street-car.

Moreover the luggage had been tumbled in

without check or paster, and Patty wondered if anybody ever could pick out their own again.

"Your regular first-class coaches are funny enough," she said to Lady Hamilton, "but they are comfortable. This box we're in is like a cattle pen."

"Oh, no," laughed Lady Hamilton; "this isn't bad at all. You see it's only a tiny branch road, running to some little hamlets, and it's not much used. There are only about two trains each way every day."

This gave Patty a different idea of the little railroad, and she began to feel a more personal interest in it. They rolled slowly through the hop-growing country, and though the scenery was not grand, it was picturesque. Patty said it was like a panorama of "The Angelus." They reached their station at about five o'clock, and found a fine open barouche awaiting them, and a wagon for their trunks.

The footman greeted them deferentially, and asked them to pick out their luggage from the lot that had been dumped on the station platform.

"I can't see either of my trunks," said Patty. "So I suppose I'd better take the ones I like best of these others."

"Nonsense," said Lady Hamilton; "yours

must be here somewhere. Look around, Marie;
you know Miss Fairfield's boxes."

" Yes, my Lady; but they are not here."

Sure enough, they weren't there, and as Patty
was certain they had been put on the train, she
concluded they had been carried on.

" What can I do? " she cried. " Can we telephone to the next station and have them sent
back? "

But in that small station, merely a tiny box,
there was no telephone.

The impassive coachman and footman from
Herenden Hall seemed to have no advice to
offer, so there was nothing to do but to proceed
to the house.

Patty was distressed at the outlook.

" Oh, Kitty," she said; " I can't go to dinner
at all! Of course I couldn't appear in this
travelling costume, and I'll have to put on one
of your négligées, and eat dinner all alone in
my room! "

The prospect was appalling, but neither of
them could think of any help for it.

" Has Lady Herenden any daughters about my
age? " Patty asked, after a few moments'
thought.

" No, indeed. She and Lord Herenden have

no children. But if there are any young girls there as guests, you might borrow a frock for to-night. Surely they'll get your things by to-morrow."

They drove into the park, through great gates, and past various lodges. The wonderful old trees waved above their heads; the marvellous lawns stretched away in rolling slopes; and the well-kept road wound along, now over a bridge, now under an arch until they paused at the noble old entrance of Herenden Hall.

Liveried servants seemed to appear, as if by magic, from all directions at once. Dogs came, barking a noisy welcome, and, following Lady Hamilton across the terrace and into the great entrance hall, Patty found herself being presented to a lovely young woman, almost as beautiful as Lady Hamilton herself.

"You must be the greatest chums," Lady Hamilton was saying, "for Miss Fairfield is one of my dearest friends, and I want you to adore each other."

"We will!" said Lady Herenden and Patty, at the same moment, and then they all laughed, and the guests were at once shown to their rooms.

After a bewildering route through several

branching halls, Patty found that to her had been assigned a large and pleasant room, which looked out upon the rose-garden. On one side it communicated with Lady Hamilton's room, and on the other opened into a dainty dressing-room and bath. It was all enchanting, and Patty's gaze rested admiringly upon the chintz draperies and Dresden ornaments, when she heard a tap at her door. Answering, she found a trim maid, who courtesied and said: " I'm Susan, Miss. Will you give me the keys of your boxes, and I'll unpack them."

Patty almost laughed at this casual request, in the face of what seemed to her a tragedy.

" Susan," she said, " here are the keys, but you can't unpack my boxes for they haven't come."

" Lor', Miss; they must be downstairs. I'll have them sent up."

" No—wait, Susan; they're not downstairs. They didn't come on the train."

" Lor ', Miss, whatever will you do? "

The girl's eyes grew big and troubled. Here was a dreadful situation indeed! Already Susan felt drawn toward the pretty young American girl, and she was aghast at the outlook of a dinner party with no party frock.

Herenden Hall

"I can't go to dinner at all, Susan," said Patty, dejectedly. "You must bring me a tray up here—though I don't feel like eating."

"Not go to dinner, Miss? Oh, what a pity! It's a grand dinner to-night. The Earl of Ruthven is here, and it's one of her ladyship's greatest dinners of the season."

The good Susan looked so concerned, and her face was so anxious, that it went straight to Patty's heart. To her mind there came a vivid and tantalising remembrance of her exquisite dinner frock, of white chiffon, embroidered with tiny sprays of blossoms—a soft sash and shoulder-knots—one of the loveliest dresses she had ever had, and with a sob she threw herself on to the couch and indulged in a few foolish but comforting tears.

"There, there, Miss," said Susan, sympathisingly, "don't ee take on so. Maybe we can find summat for ee."

When Susan was excited or troubled, she lapsed into her old dialect, which she was striving to outgrow.

"You can't find anything, I know," said Patty, sitting up, and looking the picture of woe. "There are no very young ladies in the house, are there, Susan?"

"No, Miss, none so young as yourself, nor near it."

"And I can't wear this," went on Patty, looking at the silk blouse that was part of her travelling gown.

"Lor' no, Miss; not to a dinner!"

"Then what?"

"Then what, indeed, Miss!"

Patty and Susan faced each other, at last in a full realisation of the hopelessness of the situation, when, after a light tap at the door, Lady Hamilton came in.

She laughed outright at the tragic attitude of the two, and knew at once what they were troubled about.

"Listen to me, Pattypet," she said. "Am I your fairy godmother, or am I not?"

"You are," said Patty, with an air of conviction, and feeling sure that Lady Hamilton was about to help her out of her troubles, somehow.

"Well, I've carefully considered the case. I've sent Marie to canvass the house for clothes suitable for a mademoiselle of seventeen."

"Nearly eighteen," murmured Patty.

"It doesn't matter. There isn't what's known as a ' misses' costume ' beneath this roof. Now,

Herenden Hall

I simply refuse to let you be absent from this dinner. It will be both a pleasure and an education to you to see this especial kind of a formal function, and probably you'll not often have a chance. They've sent a man and a wagon over to the next station, several miles away for your boxes; that's the way they do things here. But he can't get back until long after the dinner hour. So listen, to my command, dictum, fiat—call it what you please, but this is what you're to do."

" I'll do anything you say, Kitty Lady, if it's to go to bed at once, and sleep soundly till morning."

" Nothing of the sort. You must and shall attend this dinner. And—you're going to wear one of my gowns! "

" Yours? "

" Yes. We're so nearly the same size that it will fit you quite well enough. I've picked out the simplest one, a white Irish point. It's cut princess, but all my gowns are. I'm sure Marie can make it fit you perfectly, with a few pins or a stitch here and there."

" Oh, it will fit well enough, but, Kitty, won't I be the grown-up! I've never worn a real train in my life! "

"Of course it's a lot too old for you, and truly, I hate to have you appear in a gown like that. But what else can we do? I won't let you miss the dinner—and after all, it doesn't matter so much. After this visit I doubt if you'll ever see these people again, and let them think you're five or six years older than you are. Who cares?"

"I don't," said Patty, gleefully. "I think it will be fun. I'll have my hair piled high on my head. Can you do it for me, Sarah?"

"Oh, yes, Miss, I'm a hair-dresser and I'm that glad you're going to dinner."

CHAPTER VII

FOR ONE NIGHT ONLY

SARAH was indeed an expert hair-dresser, and she piled up Patty's hair in soft coils, and twisted the curly tendrils into fluffy puffs, and though the result was beautiful, it made Patty look like her own older sister. A jewelled ornament of Lady Hamilton's crowned the coiffure, and this gave an added effect of dignity. The lace gown was easily made to fit its new wearer. Marie pinned it, and sewed it, and patted it into place, till nobody would suspect it had not been made for Patty. But the long lines of the Princess pattern took away all of Patty's usual simple girlish appearance, and transformed her at once into a beautiful, queenly young woman. The décolletée corsage, and the sleeves, which were merely frills of lace, were very becoming; and the long train, which billowed into a frou-frou of chiffon ruffles took away the last semblance of a girl of eighteen. Notwithstanding her softly-curved cheeks and throat, and her exquisite, fresh complexion,

Patty's Friends

Patty looked quite the young woman of society and could easily have been adjudged about twenty-four years old.

Her eyes danced, as she walked sedately through the open door and into Lady Hamilton's room.

"My word, Patty!" exclaimed that lady, "you're simply stunning in that gown! You look as if you'd been 'out' for two or three seasons. Your people would never forgive me if they knew how I've dressed you up."

"It was the only thing to do," said Patty, airily, as she began to draw on her arms a pair of Lady Hamilton's long white gloves. "The wonder is that you had plenty of all sorts of things to fit me out, and also that they do fit so well. These gloves are just right, though I confess the slippers pinch me just a speck."

"'Pretty never hurts,' you know," said Lady Hamilton, laughing. "Marie, isn't Miss Fairfield a picture?"

"*Mais oui!* She is *charmante*. It is amazing how the gown suits her. She is *très-belle!*"

With the grown-up clothes, Patty had, quite unconsciously assumed a grown-up air. She nonchalantly flung aside her train with just the same gesture Lady Hamilton was wont to use,

and she carried herself with a dignity and gra-
ciousness of manner which would have been absurd when wearing her own simple frocks.

" Gracious, goodness, child! " cried Lady
Hamilton. " Come down off that pedestal!
You walk like a Duchess. It won't do, you
know, really."

" I don't mean to," said Patty; " you know I'm
a sort of chameleon. This gown makes me feel
as if I belonged in an opera-box, or had an audience with the Queen."

" Oh, you goose! Stop your nonsense, and
we'll go down to dinner. Mind, now, none of
those airs, or I'll send you back to your room."

Patty honestly tried to be her own simple-
minded self, and would have succeeded all right,
if Herenden Hall had not been so lavishly pro-
vided with mirrors. On the grand staircase she
came face to face with a radiant creature, and
was about to step aside when she discovered it
was herself! Involuntarily she gazed at the reflection of the white-gowned lady, and unconsciously an air of serenity, almost hauteur, replaced her usual merry smile, and with a gracious mien she passed on down the stairs.

Lady Herenden awaited them in the drawing-
room.

Patty's Friends

A brilliant assemblage was already there, for Patty's unusual costuming had caused her some delay. After the first few introductions, Lady Hamilton and Patty became separated, and the guests stood about conversing in small groups.

Patty chanced to fall in with some very entertaining people, among whom was the Earl of Ruthven.

The Earl was a handsome man, tall, and of an imposing presence.

When presented to Patty, he gazed at her with frank, though quite deferential admiration. "So pleased to meet you, Miss Fairfield," he said; "I adore American ladies."

Patty really felt a little in awe of an Earl, as she had never met one before, and was about to make a shy response, when a slight movement of her head showed her her own reflection in a near-by mirror.

Realising afresh that she was masquerading as a society lady, a spirit of mischief suddenly took possession of her, and she determined to throw herself into the rôle. So, with a pretty little toss of her head, and a charming smile, she said:

"Thank you, Lord Ruthven; I adore Englishmen, too, but I know so few of them."

For One Night Only

" You've not been here long, then? "

" No, only a few weeks. And there's so much I want to learn."

" Let me teach you," said his Lordship, eagerly. " I do not think you would prove a dull pupil."

Patty's eyes smiled. " No Americans are dull," she said.

" That's true; my experience has already proved it. I've met six, I think, including yourself. But what sort of things do you want to learn? "

" The language, principally. I just want to learn to say ' only fancy ' occasionally, and ' d'y' see? ' in the middle of every sentence."

" It's not easy," said Lord Ruthven, thoughtfully, " but I think I can teach you in, say, about ten lessons. When shall we begin the course? "

Patty looked at him reproachfully. " If you knew the American nature at all," she said, " you'd know that we always begin things the moment the plan occurs to us."

" Good! there's no time like the present."

But just then their conversation was interrupted by the announcement of dinner.

Patty hoped she would sit at table next the Earl, but it was not so. The nobleman was accorded the seat of honour at the right of his hostess, while Patty, as a minor guest, was far away across the table. But she found herself between two affable and pleasant-mannered young Englishmen, and instantly forgot all about her titled friend.

Indeed, the bewildering beauty of the scene claimed her attention, and she fairly held her breath as she looked about her. The great oval room was lighted only by wax candles in crystal chandeliers and candelabra. This made a soft, mellow radiance quite different from gas or electricity. On one side of the room long French windows opened on to the terrace, through which came the scent of roses and the sound of plashing fountains. On the other side, only slender pillars and arches divided the dining-room from a conservatory, and a riotous tangle of blossoms and foliage fairly spilled into the room, forming almost a cascade of flowers.

The great round table was a bewildering array of gold plate, gilded glass, and exquisite china, while on the delicate lace of the tablecloth lay rare blossoms that seemed to have drifted from the circular mound of flowers which formed the low centrepiece.

Twenty-four guests sat round the board, in

chairs of gilded wicker, and as the silent, black-garbed waiters served the viands, the scene became as animated as it was beautiful.

Patty forgot all else in her absolute enjoyment of the fairy-like spectacle, and was only brought back to a sense of reality by the sound of a voice at her side. Mr. Merivale was speaking—the young man who had escorted her out to dinner, and who now sat at her right hand.

"You love beauty of detail," he was saying as he noted Patty's absorption.

"Oh, isn't it great!" she exclaimed, and then suddenly realised that the expression was not at all in keeping with the dignity of her Princess gown.

But Mr. Merivale seemed amused rather than shocked.

"That's American for 'ripping,' isn't it?" he said, smiling. "But whatever the adjective, the fact is the same. Lady Herenden's dinners are always the refinement of the spectacular."

Patty realised the appropriateness of this phrase, and cudgelled her brain for an appropriate reply. She began to think that playing grown-up was a more difficult game than she had supposed. Had she had on her own simple little frock, Mr. Merivale would not have talked to her like that.

"Don't you remember last season," he went on, "when Lady Herenden had a real pond, with gold fish in the middle of the table, and ferns and water lilies round the edge?"

"I wasn't here last season," said Patty. "I have never been in England until this summer."

"Indeed? I know you are an American, but you have really an English manner."

"It's acquired," said Patty, with a mischievous twinkle in her eye. "I find my American manner isn't admired over here, so I assume London airs."

"Ah, you wish to be admired?"

"Of all things!" declared naughty Patty, with a roguish glance at the jesting young man.

"You'll probably get your wish," he replied. "I'm jolly well ready to do my share."

This brought the colour to Patty's cheeks, and she turned slightly away, toward the man on her other side.

He was a slightly older man than Mr. Merivale and was the squire of an adjoining estate. He was quite ready to talk to his American neighbour, and began the conversation by asking her if she had yet seen Lady Herenden's rose-orchard.

"No, Mr. Snowden," said Patty, "I only arrived a few hours ago, and I've not been round the place at all."

"Then let me show it to you, please. I'll come over to-morrow morning for a stroll. May I?"

"I don't know," said Patty, hesitatingly, for she was uncertain what she ought to do in the matter. "You see, I'm with Lady Hamilton, and whatever she says——"

"Oh, nonsense! She'll spare you from her side for an hour or two. There's really a lot to see."

Again poor Patty realised her anomalous position. But for her piled-up hair and her trained gown, the man would never have dreamed of asking her to go for a walk unchaperoned. Patty had learned the ethics of London etiquette for girls of eighteen, but she was not versed in the ways of older young women.

"We'll see about it," she said, non-committally, and then she almost laughed outright at the sudden thought of Mr. Snowden's surprise should he see her next day in one of her own simple morning frocks of light muslin. Lady

Hamilton's morning gowns were Paris affairs, with trailing frills and long knotted ribbons.

"It seems to amuse you," said Mr. Snowden, a trifle piqued at her merriment.

"You'll be amused, too," she said, "if you see me to-morrow."

Then something in the man's pleasant face seemed to invite confidence, and she said, impulsively:

"I may as well tell you that I'm masquerading. I'm not a grown-up lady at all. I'm not much more than a schoolgirl—not quite eighteen years old. But—but my box didn't come, and —and I had to wear Lady Hamilton's gown. It makes me seem a lot older, I know, but I had to do it, or stay away from dinner."

Mr. Snowden looked first amazed, and then he burst into laughter.

"I beg your pardon, I'm sure," he said, "but I had no idea! And so Lady Hamilton is your chaperon? I see. Of course. Well, we'll have the stroll just the same, if you will, and we'll ask her to go with us."

"Isn't she the dearest thing?" exclaimed Patty, looking at Lady Kitty across the table, and feeling much more at her ease now that she had confessed her position.

For One Night Only

"She is a beautiful and charming woman," agreed Mr. Snowden.

And then it was time for Patty to turn back to Mr. Merivale, for she had learned that one must divide the time fairly between dinner neighbors.

"I didn't offend you, did I?" said young Merivale, eagerly. "You turned so quickly—and—and you—er—blushed, you know, and so I was afraid—er——"

But Patty was of no mind to confess the fewness of her years to everybody, and her mischievous spirit returned as she determined to chaff this amusing young man.

"What!" she said, reproachfully, "an Englishman, and afraid!"

"Afraid of nothing but a fair lady's displeasure. All true Englishmen surrender to that."

"I'm not displeased," said Patty, dimpling and smiling; "in fact, I've even forgotten what you said."

"That's good! Now we can start fresh. Will you save a lot of dances for me to-night?"

"Oh, will there be dancing?" exclaimed Patty, delighted at the prospect.

"Yes, indeed; in the big ballroom. Will you give me all the waltzes?"

Patty looked at him in amazement. "You said you were going to 'start fresh,'" she said, "and now you've certainly done so!"

But the American phrase was lost on the Englishman, who only proceeded to repeat his request.

Meantime, Mr. Snowden was asking Patty for a dance.

"Certainly," she said, "I shall be pleased to dance with you."

"You'll give me more than one dance or you needn't give me any," grumbled young Merivale.

"All right," said Patty, quickly. "Mr. Snowden, I've just had a dance 'returned with thanks,' so you can have that, if you wish it."

"I do indeed," he replied, enthusiastically, and Mr. Merivale relapsed into a sulky silence.

Then Lady Herenden rose from the table, and the ladies all rose and followed her up to one of the beautiful salons, where coffee was served to them. Patty managed to secure a seat on a divan beside Lady Hamilton.

"You quite take my breath away, little Patty," said her friend, in a low voice. "You are already a favourite, and in a fair way to become the belle of the ball."

For One Night Only

"I try not to act too old, Kitty," said Patty, earnestly, "but truly everybody thinks I'm a society lady. They don't even look on me as a débutante."

"Never mind, dearie; have all the fun you can. Enjoy the dancing, and don't care what anybody thinks."

Encouraged by Lady Hamilton's approval, Patty ceased to think about her demeanour and proceeded to enjoy the conversation of those about her.

Lady Herenden was especially kind to her, and singled out the young American for her special favour and attention.

CHAPTER VIII

THE EARL OF RUTHVEN

AFTER a time the men came from the dining-room and rejoined the ladies.

Patty was chatting with a group of young women, and when she glanced around, it was to see Lord Ruthven standing at her side.

"I was miles away from you at dinner," he said, "but now there is an opportunity, let us begin our lessons in English at once."

"Do," said Patty, smiling; "where shall be our classroom?"

"We'll pre-empt this sofa," said Lord Ruthven, indicating, as he spoke, a gold-framed Louis XIV. tête-à-tête. "We'll pretend that it is a real schoolroom, with four walls hung with maps and charts—just such as you used to have when you were a little girl."

Patty smiled at this reference to her far-away school-days, but fell in with his mood.

"Yes," she said, "and you must be the stern schoolmaster, and I the stupid pupil who has been kept in after school."

The Earl of Ruthven

But their merry game was interrupted by Lady Herenden's invitation to the ballroom.

Escorted by Lord Ruthven, Patty followed the others to the great hall where they were to dance.

It was a resplendent apartment, with balconies and boxes, from which the spectators could look down upon the dancers. A fine orchestra furnished the music, and Patty, who loved to dance, found her feet involuntarily keeping time to the harmonious strains.

"Shall we have a try?" said Lord Ruthven, and in a moment they were gliding over the smooth floor.

Patty already knew that English dancing is not like the American steps, but she was so completely mistress of the art, that she could adapt herself instantly to any variation.

"I won't compliment your dancing," said the Earl, as the waltz was finished, "for you must have been told so often how wonderfully well you dance. But I must tell you what a pleasure it is to dance with you."

Patty thought this a very pretty speech, and graciously gave his lordship some other dances for which he asked, and then, leaving her with Lady Herenden, he excused himself and went away. Then Patty was besieged with would-be partners. Her dancing had called forth the admiration of everybody, and the young men crowded about, begging to see her dance-card.

Only Mr. Merivale stood aloof. He was still sulky, and he looked so like a cross schoolboy that Patty took pity on him.

She slightly nodded her head at him by way of invitation, and he came slowly toward her.

"Which two do you want?" she said, demurely.

Merivale's face lighted up. "You are indeed kind," he said, in a low voice. "I will take any you will give me. My card is blank as yet."

So Patty arranged the dances, and the young man went away looking much happier. The evening was all too short. Patty whirled through dance after dance, and between them was restored to Lady Herenden or Lady Hamilton, only to be claimed the next minute by another partner.

"What a belle it is!" said Lady Herenden, patting the girl's shoulder affectionately. "You have made a real sensation, Miss Fairfield."

"But I'm Cinderella, to-night," she said, gaily.

The Earl of Ruthven

" Wait till to-morrow, and see all my popularity vanish."

Lady Herenden did not understand, but took it as merry chaff and paid no heed.

Then Lord Ruthven came for the last dance.

" This is an extra, Miss Fairfield," he said; " will you give it to me? "

Patty agreed, but as they walked away, his Lordship said:

" You look really tired; would you not rather sit on the terrace than dance? "

" I am tired," said Patty, honestly; " I think it's carrying this heavy train around. I've never before danced in a long gown."

" Then you shall rest. Let us sit on the terrace, and I'll send for an ice for you."

Lord Ruthven was very kind and courteous. He found a delightful corner of the terrace unoccupied, and he arranged two wicker easychairs, where they might be just out of the way of the promenaders. He asked a footman to bring the ices, and then seated himself beside Patty.

" Is it not beautiful," he said, " the rose garden in the moonlight? One can almost fancy the roses opening beneath the moon's light as in daytime by the sun's warm rays."

Patty's Friends

" Yes," said Patty, falling in with his fanciful mood, " and I think, perhaps, at night, the white roses and the pale yellow ones bloom. Then at daybreak, the pink or blush roses open, and at midday the deep red ones."

" You have the mind of a poet, Miss Fairfield. Where do you get those graceful conceits? "

" Oh, I don't know," said Patty, carelessly; " I think they are the result of this beautiful moonlight night, and these picturesque surroundings."

" Yes, I am sure that is true. You have a soul that responds to all beauty in art or nature. Let us take a short turn in the rose garden, and get a view of this noble old house with the moonlight full upon it."

" But I want my ice cream," objected Patty, who still had her schoolgirl appetite.

" We'll stay but a moment, and we'll return to find it awaiting us," gently insisted Lord Ruthven, and Patty amiably went down the terrace steps and along the garden path with him.

Near a clump of cedars, only a short distance away, they turned to look at the beautiful old house. Herenden Hall was always a splendid picture, but especially at night, backgrounded by a gray sky full of racing clouds, and touched at every gable by the silver moonlight, it was enchanting.

" Oh," said Patty, drawing a sigh, " it is the most wonderful effect I ever saw. See that great, quiet roof sloping darkly away, and beneath, the gay lights of the terrace, and the laughter of happy people."

" It is a beautiful picture," said Lord Ruthven, looking steadily at Patty, " but not so beautiful as another one I see. A lovely face framed in soft, shining curls, against a background of dark cedar trees."

His tone, even more than his words, alarmed Patty. She was not used to such speeches as this, and she said, gravely: " Take me back to the house, please, Lord Ruthven."

" Not just yet," pleaded the nobleman. " Dear Miss Fairfield, listen to me a moment. Let me tell you something. Let me justify myself. I oughtn't to talk to you like this, I know—but the fact is—oh, the fact is you've completely bowled me over."

" What? " said Patty, not at all comprehending his meaning.

" Yes; I'm done for—and at first sight! And by an American! But it's a fact. I adore you,

Patty's Friends

'Miss Fairfield—I'm so desperately in love with you that I can't down it. Oh, I know I oughtn't to be talking to you like this. I ought to see your father, and all that. And I will, as soon as I can, but—oh, I say, Patty, tell me you like me a little! "

It suddenly dawned on Patty that she was having a proposal! And from an English Earl! And all on account of her grown-up gown! The absurdity of it impressed her far more than the romantic side of it, and though a little frightened, she couldn't help smiling at the Earl's tragic tones.

" Nonsense, Lord Ruthven," she said, though her cheeks were pink; " don't talk like that. Please cut me that lovely cluster of roses, and then take me back to Lady Hamilton."

The Earl drew a penknife from his pocket, and cut the flowers she asked for. Then he stood, trimming off the thorns, and looking down at her.

Patty had never looked so winsome. Her garb made her seem a grown woman, and yet the situation alarmed her, and her perplexed face was that of a troubled child.

" Tell me," he repeated, " that you like me a little."

The Earl of Ruthven

" Of course I like you a little," returned Patty, in a matter-of-fact voice. " Why shouldn't I ? "

" That's something," said the Earl, in a tone of satisfaction, " and now will you accept these flowers as a gift from me? As, for the moment, I've nothing else to offer."

Patty took the flowers in both hands, but Lord Ruthven still held them, too, saying: " And will you let them mean——"

" No," cried Patty, " they don't mean anything —not anything at all! "

Lord Ruthven clasped Patty's two hands, roses and all, in his own.

" They do," he said quietly; " they mean I love you. Do you understand? "

He looked straight into the troubled, beseeching eyes that met his own.

" Please let me go, Lord Ruthven—*please!* " said Patty, her hands trembling in his own.

" You may go, if you will first call me by some less formal name. Patty, dearest, say Sylvester —just once! "

This desperate request was too much for Patty's sense of humour.

" Why can't I say it twice? " she said in a low tone, but her voice was shaking with laughter.

"You little witch!" exclaimed the Earl, and his clasp tightened on her hands. "Now you shan't go until you *have* said it twice!"

"Sylvester—Sylvester—there!" said Patty, her eyes twinkling with fun, and her lips on the verge of laughter. Then, gently disengaging her hands from his, she gathered up her long white train, and prepared to run away.

The Earl laid a detaining hand on her arm. "Miss Fairfield," he said, "Patty, I won't keep you now, but to-morrow you'll give me an opportunity, won't you? to tell you——"

"Wait till to-morrow, my lord," said Patty, really laughing now. "You will probably have changed your mind."

"How little you know me!" he cried, reproachfully, and then they had reached the terrace, and joined the others.

Soon after the guests all retired to their own rooms, and the moonlight on Herenden Hall saw no more the gay scene on the terrace.

Patty, passing through her own room, discovered that her two trunks had arrived and had been unpacked. She went straight on and tapped at Lady Hamilton's door. "Get me out of this gown, please, Marie; I've had quite enough of being a grown-up young woman!"

The Earl of Ruthven

" What's the matter, Patty? " said Lady Kitty, looking round. " Didn't you have a good time this evening? "

" The time of my life! " declared Patty, dropping into her own graphic speech, as she emerged from the heap of lace and silk. " I'll see you later, Kitty," and without further word she returned to her own room.

And later, when Marie had been dismissed, Patty crept back to Lady Hamilton, a very different Patty, indeed. Her hair fell in two long braids, with curly tails; a dainty dressing-gown, enveloped her slight figure; and on her bare feet were heelless satin slippers. She found Lady Kitty in an armchair before the wood fire, awaiting her.

Patty threw a big, fat sofa pillow at her friend's feet, and settled herself cosily upon it.

" Well, girlie," said Lady Hamilton, " come to the story at once. What happened to you as a grown-up? "

" What usually happens to grown-ups, I suppose," said Patty, demurely; " the Earl of Ruthven proposed to me."

" What! " cried Lady Hamilton, starting up, and quite upsetting Patty from her cushion.

" Yes, he did," went on Patty, placidly; " shall I accept him? "

" Patty, you naughty child, tell me all about it at once! Oh, what shall I say to your father and mother? "

Patty grinned. " Yes, it was all your fault, Kitty. If I hadn't worn your gown, he would never have dreamed of such a thing."

" But, Patty, it *can't* be true. You must have misunderstood him."

" Not I. It's my first proposal, to be sure; but I know what a man means when he says he loves me and begs me to call him by his first name. And I did—twice."

Patty went off in shrieks of laughter at the remembrance of it, and she rocked back and forth on her cushion in paroxysms of mirth.

" Patty, behave yourself, and tell me the truth. I've a mind to shake you! "

" I *am* shaking," said Patty, trying to control her voice. " And I *am* telling you the truth. His first name is Sylvester. Lovely name! "

" Where did this occur? "

" In the rose garden. Oh, right near the terrace. Not a dozen yards away from you all.

I'm sure if you'd been listening, you could have
heard me say, ' Sylvester—*Sylvester!* ' "

Again Patty went off in uncontrollable merriment at this recollection, and Lady Kitty had to
laugh too.

" What did you tell him? "

" I told him to wait till to-morrow, and he'd
probably change his mind. And I see my trunks
have come, so he surely will. You see he proposed to that long-tailed gown and jewelled
tiara I had on——"

" It wasn't a tiara."

" Well, it looked something like one. I'm sure
he thought it was. He doubtless wants a dignified, stately Lady Ruthven, and he thought
I was *it*. Oh, Kitty! if you could have heard
him."

" I don't think it's nice of you, to take him
that way."

" All right, I won't. But I'm not going to
take him at all. Why, Kitty, when he sees me
to-morrow in my own little pink muslin, he
won't know me, let alone remembering what he
said to me."

" Patty, you're incorrigible. I don't know
what to say to you. But I hope your parents
won't blame me for this."

[117]

Patty's Friends

"Of course they won't, Kitsie. You see it was an accident. A sort of case of mistaken identity. I don't mind it so much now that it's over, but I was scared stiff at the time. Only it was all so funny that it swallowed up my scare. Now I'll tell you the whole story."

So Patty told every word that the Earl had said to her during the evening, in the ballroom and on the terrace. And Lady Hamilton listened attentively.

"You were not a bit to blame, dear," she said, kindly, when the tale was finished. "I don't think you even flirted with him. But it's truly extraordinary that he should speak so soon."

"It was on the spur of the moment," declared Patty, with conviction. "You know, moonlight and roses and a summer evening have a romantic influence on some natures."

"What do you know of a romantic influence, you baby. Hop along to bed, now, and get up in the morning your own sweet, natural self—without a thought of Earls or moonlight."

"I will so," said Patty; "I didn't like it a bit, except that it was all so funny. Won't Nan howl?"

"She may, but I'm afraid your father will be annoyed. You know you're in my care, Patty."

"Don't you worry. I'll tell Daddy all about it. And I rather guess it will make him laugh."

CHAPTER IX

AN IMPORTANT DOCUMENT

IT was the custom at Herenden Hall to serve morning tea to the guests in their rooms.

When Patty's tray was brought, she asked to have it taken into Lady Hamilton's room, and the two friends chatted cosily over their toast and teacups.

Lady Kitty, with a dainty dressing-jacket round her shoulders, was still nestled among her pillows, while Patty, in a blue kimono, curled up, Turk-fashion on the foot of the bed.

" It's a gorgeous day," observed Patty, stirring her tea, which she was trying to sip, though she hated it. " I'll be glad to explore that lovely rose garden without horrid old moonlit Earls."

" It's a wonderfully fine place, Patty; you really must go over the estate. I'll show you round myself."

" Thank you," said Patty, airily, " but I believe I have an engagement. Mr. Snowden, or Snowed on, or Snowed under, or whatever his name is, kindly offered to do that same."

An Important Document

" Yes, and he'll kindly withdraw his offer when he sees you in your own rightful raiment. I've a notion to put you in a pinafore, and give you a Teddy Bear to carry. There's no keeping you down any other way."

" Oh, don't be alarmed. I've no designs on the young men. I like the boys better, anyhow. That Jack Merivale is a chummy kind of a youth. That's the sort I like. Rest assured I won't trouble that wretched Earl. I won't even speak to him, and I'll make over to you whatever interest he may deign to show in me."

" As one Humpty Dumpty said, ' I'd rather see that on paper.' "

" So you shall," said Patty, and setting down her unfinished tea, she flew to the writing table.

Perching herself on the corner of the desk chair, she laid out a sheet of Lady Herenden's crested note paper, and took up a pen. " Shall I write the agreement as I please? " she said, " or will you dictate it? "

" I'll dictate," said Lady Kitty, smiling lazily at the foolery. But as she paused between sentences, Patty put in parentheses of her own, and when finished the remarkable document read thus:

Patty's Friends

"I, the undersigned, being of (fairly) sound mind, do hereby of my own free will (coerced by one Lady Hamilton) relinquish all interest or concern in the (illustrious) personage known as Sylvester, Earl of Ruthven (but I do think he has a lovely name), and should he show any interest in me, personally, I promise (gladly) to refer him to (the aforesaid) Lady Hamilton (though what she wants of him, I don't know!), and I hereby solemnly promise and agree, not to seek or accept any further acquaintance or friendship with the (Belted) gentleman above referred to.

"Furthermore, I (being still of sound mind, but it's tottering) promise not to talk or converse with the (Sylvester! *Sylvester!*) Earl of Ruthven, beyond the ordinary civilities of the day (whatever that may mean!), never to smile at him voluntarily (I can't help laughing at him), and *never* to wave my eyelashes at him across the table. (*Why* does she think I'd do that?)

"Witness my hand and seal,

"PATRICIA FAIRFIELD."

("Lady Patricia would **sound great!** Wouldn't it?")

An Important Document

"There, Kitty Cat," said Patty, tossing the paper to Lady Hamilton, "there's your agreement, and now, my dreams of glory over, I'll go and 'bind my hair and lace my bodice blue.' I always wondered how people bind their hair. Do you suppose they use skirt braid?"

But Lady Kitty was shaking with laughter over Patty's foolish "document" and offered no reply.

An hour or so later, Patty presented herself for inspection.

She wore a pale blue dimity, whose round, full blouse was belted with a soft ribbon. The skirt, with its three frills edged with tiny lace, came just to her instep, and disclosed dainty, patent-leather oxfords.

Her golden braids, crossed and recrossed low at the back of her head, were almost covered by a big butterfly bow of wide white ribbon. In fact, she was perfectly garbed for an American girl of eighteen, and the costume was more becoming to her pretty, young face than the trained gown of the night before.

Lady Hamilton was still at her dressing table.

"I feel quite at ease about you now," she said, looking up. "Nobody will propose to you in that rig. They'll be more likely to buy you a doll. I'm not nearly ready yet, but don't wait. Run along downstairs, you'll find plenty of people about."

Slowly Patty descended the great staircase, looking at the pictures and hanging rugs as she passed them.

"For mercy's sake, who is that?" was Lady Herenden's mental exclamation as the girl neared the lower floor.

"Good-morning, Lady Herenden," cried Patty, gaily, as she approached her hostess. "Don't look so surprised to see me, and I'll tell you all about it."

"Why, it's Miss Fairfield!" exclaimed the elder lady, making room for Patty on the sofa beside her.

"Yes, and I really owe you an explanation. You see, my boxes didn't come last night, and I had to wear one of Lady Hamilton's gowns at dinner. I couldn't tell you so, before all the guests, and so you didn't know me this morning in my own frock."

"It's astonishing what a difference it makes! You look years younger."

"I am. I'm not quite eighteen yet, and I wish you'd call me Patty, won't you?"

"I will, indeed," said Lady Herenden, answering the pretty smile that accompanied the request. " I knew Kitty Hamilton said you weren't out yet, and so, when I saw you last night, I just couldn't understand it. But I do now. Have you breakfasted, dearie? "

" Yes, thank you. And now, I want to go out and see the flowers, and the dogs. May I? "

" Yes, indeed. Run around as you like. You'll find people on the terrace and lawn, though there are no girls here as young as yourself."

" That doesn't matter. I like people of all ages. I've friends from four to forty."

" I'm not surprised. You're a friendly little thing. Be sure to go through the rose orchard; it's back of the rose garden, and you'll love it."

Hatless, Patty ran out into the sunshine, and, strolling through the rose garden, soon forgot all else in her delight at the marvellous array of blossoms.

As she turned a corner of a path, she came upon two men talking together. They were Lord Ruthven and Lord Herenden's head gardener.

" Yes," his lordship was saying, " you've done a good thing, Parker, in getting that hybrid.

And this next bush is a fine one, too. Is it a Baroness Rothschild? "

" No," said Patty, carelessly joining in the conversation, " it's a Catherine Mermet."

" So it is, Miss," said the gardener, turning politely toward her, but Lord Ruthven, after a slight glance, paid no attention to the girl.

" Are you sure, Parker? " he said. " The Mermets are usually pinker."

" He doesn't know me! What larks! " thought Patty, gleefully. " I'll try again."

" Where is the rose orchard, Parker? " she asked, turning her full face toward the gardener, and leaving only the big white bow to greet the Earl.

Something in her voice startled Lord Ruthven, and he wheeled quickly about. " It is—it can't be—Miss Fairfield? "

" Good-morning, my lord," said Patty, with cool politeness. " This, of course," she thought to herself, " is the civility of the day."

" I will show you the rose orchard," went on the Earl. " Come with me."

" No, thank you," said Patty, turning again to the gardener. She was absurdly placed, and she felt a little embarrassed. But, on the other hand, she had pledged her word, and a silly performance it was! But she would keep it, at least until Lady Hamilton released her from her promise. Patty's ideas of honour were, perhaps, a little strained, but she took the promise of that burlesque document as seriously as if it had been of national importance. And now she was in a dilemma. To refuse to walk with the Earl was so rude, and yet to talk with him was to break her pledged word.

The gardener went on about his work, and the other two stood silent. For the first time in her life, Patty had a really difficult situation to cope with. If she could have laughed and talked naturally, it would have been easy to explain matters. But that absurd paper sealed her lips. Oh, why had she been so foolish?

She did not look at the Earl, but he gazed fixedly at her.

" I don't understand," he said. " Why are you so changed from last evening? "

Patty thought hard. She was allowed the civilities of the day," so she must depend on those.

" Isn't it a charming morning? " she said, without, however, turning toward the man at her side.

"It is indeed. But why are you such an enigma? Are all Americans so puzzling?"

"And isn't the rose garden wonderful?" went on Patty, still looking off in the distance.

"Wonderful, of course. Please look at me. I believe, after all, you're Miss Fairfield's younger sister! Ah, I have guessed you at last!"

Patty still looked straight ahead, but an irrepressible smile dimpled the corners of her mouth.

"Do you think it will rain?" she said.

"By Jove, I won't stand this!" cried the Earl, impetuously. "I know you are yourself—the Miss Fairfield I talked with last night—but why you're masquerading as a schoolgirl, I don't know!"

At this Patty could restrain her mirth no longer, and her pretty laughter seemed to appease the Earl's irritation.

"Am I not fit to be looked at, or spoken to?" he said, more gently; "and if not, you must at least tell me why."

"I can't tell you why," said Patty, stifling her laughter, but still gazing at the far-away hills.

"Why can't you? Have you promised not to?" The Earl meant this as a jest, little thinking it was the truth, but Patty, now nearly chok-ing with merriment, said demurely, " Yes, sir."

" Nonsense! I'm not going to eat you! Look at me, child."

" I can't," repeated Patty, in a small voice, and holding her wilful, golden head very straight, as she stared firmly ahead.

" Whom did you promise? "

" You have no right to ask."—" That," said Patty to herself, " is an ordinary *incivility,* but I can't help it! "

" I have a right to ask! And I don't care whether I have or not. You're a mischief, and I won't stand any more of your chaff. Who made you promise not to speak to me, or look at me? "

The Earl, quietly, but with a decided air, moved around until he faced Patty, and the laughing blue eyes were so full of fun that he laughed too.

" You ridiculous baby! " he cried; " what are you, anyway? One night, a charming young woman, the next day, a naughty child."

" I'm *not* naughty! Nobody made me prom-ise. I did it of my own free will."

" But whom did you promise? "

" Lady Hamilton," said Patty, remembering

all at once that the matter was to be referred to her.

"Oho! Well, now, see here. You just break that promise, as quick as you can, and I'll make it square with Lady Hamilton."

"Will you?" said Patty, drawing a long sigh of relief. "And will you blot out last evening, and pretend it never was, and begin our acquaintance from now?"

"I will," said the Earl, looking at her, curiously, "if you will tell me why you seem to have a dual personality."

Then Patty explained her appearance at dinner in Lady Hamilton's gown, and to her pleased surprise, the Earl laughed long and loudly.

"Best joke ever!" he declared; "a baby like you giving an imitation of the 'belle of the ball'!"

"I'm not so infantile," said Patty, pouting a little, for the Earl now treated her as if she were about twelve.

"You are!" he declared. "You ought to be in the schoolroom eating bread and jam."

"I'd like the bread and jam well enough, for I'm getting hungrier every minute."

"Well, it's an hour yet to luncheon time; come along and I'll show you the rose orchard. It may make you forget your gnawing pangs of hunger."

On pleasant terms, then, they went through the gate in the high hedge that surrounded the encloseure. The rose orchard was unique. It had originally been a fruit orchard, and as most of the trees were dead, and many of them fallen, roses had been trained over their trunks and branches. The gorgeous masses of bloom covered the old gnarled wood, and the climbing roses twined lovingly around branches and boughs. Here and there were rustic seats and arbours; and there were many bird-houses, whose tiny occupants were exceedingly tame and sociable. Several other guests were walking about, and Patty and the Earl joined a group which included their host and hostess.

" How do you like it? " said Lady Herenden, drawing Patty's arm through her own.

" It's the most beautiful place since the Garden of Eden," said Patty, so enthusiastically that everybody laughed.

Then Mr. Snowden sauntered up, and reminded Patty of her promise to go walking with him.

" You haven't seen the deer park yet," he said, " nor the carp pond; though I believe the carp are merely tradition. Still, the pond is there."

"Run along, child!" said Lady Herenden. "You'll just about have time for a pleasant stroll before luncheon."

Patty was greatly relieved when Mr. Snowden made no reference to her age or her costume. He treated her politely and chatted gaily as he led her around to see all the picturesque bits of woodland and meadow. The magnificent old place showed its age, for it had not been unduly renovated, though everything was in good order.

They went into the old church, which was on the estate, they visited the farmhouses and stables, and Patty found Mr. Snowden a kind and entertaining guide.

CHAPTER X

A MOMENTOUS INTERVIEW

THE rest of their stay at Herenden Hall passed off delightfully. Patty fitted into her own niche, and everybody liked the natural, unaffected young girl.

She and Jack Merivale became good chums, and went fishing together, and rowing on the pond like old cronies.

It was Patty's nature to make friends quickly, and during her stay in Kent, she had a royal good time. Lord Ruthven talked over the matter with Lady Hamilton, and as he chose to consider it all a great joke on himself, she also took his view of it. As for Patty, she was so engrossed with other people that she nearly forgot all about the moonlight episode.

Only sometimes, when she chanced to catch sight of Lord Ruthven, she would say to herself, " Sylvester, *Sylvester!* " and then turn away to hide her laughter.

They stayed over until Tuesday, and then took the noon train back to London, Lady Herenden

expressing an earnest wish that Patty would
visit her again. Lady Kitty and Patty reached
the Savoy duly, and Mr. Fairfield invited the
returned travellers to dinner in the great Restaurant. This was a treat in itself, and Patty
gleefully ran up to her room to dress for
dinner.

"Lend me one of your gowns to wear,
Kitty?" she said, roguishly, looking in at her
friend's door.

"Go away, you bad child. You're not in my
care, now. I shall confess all to your father to-
night at dinner, and then I've done with you."

"You've chosen a wise time," said Patty,
sagely. "Father's always especially good-natured at dinner."

"Let us hope he will be," said Lady Hamilton, who was really a little anxious about it all.
But she need not have been, for when the story
was told, both Mr. and Mrs. Fairfield looked
upon it as a huge joke.

Nan, especially, was almost convulsed with
laughter at the account Patty gave of the moonlight scene, and her tragic repetition in a stage
whisper of "Sylvester, *Sylvester!*" was truly
funny of itself.

"It couldn't be helped," said Mr. Fairfield,

A Momentous Interview

" and it was in no way your fault, Lady Hamilton. It would have been a pity to shut Patty in her room on such a gala occasion, and no one could foresee that she was going to throw herself at the Earl's head! "

" Father! " exclaimed Patty, " I didn't do any such thing! He threw himself at my feet, if you please."

" Well, it's all right, chickabiddy, but don't let it happen again. At least, not for many years, yet. I suppose some time, in the far future, I shall be asked to be a father-in-law to a Duke or a Count, but let's put it off as long as possible."

" Then Nan will be Dowager Duchess," cried irrepressible Patty, " won't that be fun! "

" I can do it," said Nan, with an air of self-satisfaction that made them all laugh.

" I'm glad you exonerate me," said Lady Hamilton, with a sigh of relief. " And since I let Patty appear too old, I'm going to average matters in this way. Next week is the child's birthday, and I want to give her a children's party, if I may. You and your husband may come, Mrs. Fairfield, if you'll both dress as children of tender years."

" We'll do it," cried Mr. Fairfield. " This is

an inspiration of yours, Lady Hamilton, and will, as you say, quite even things up."

Then plans were speedily made for the children's party. It was only a week to Patty's birthday, but Lady Kitty said that was long enough ahead to send invitations to an afternoon affair.

For the party was to be held from three to six, and each guest was asked to dress as a small child. Patty put considerable thought on her own costume, for she said her eighteenth birthday was an important occasion, and she must do it honour.

She finally decided on a quaint little Kate Greenaway dress, and big-brimmed hat of dark green velvet with white feathers tumbling over its brim. The frock was ankle length and short-waisted and she wore old-fashioned little slippers, with crossed ribbons, and black lace mitts. A shirred silk workbag hung at her side, and she carried a tiny parasol.

A few days before the party, Patty had an inspiration. It came to her suddenly, as most inspirations do, and it was so startling that it almost took her breath away.

" I *can't* do it," she said to herself, one minute; and " I *will* do it," she said to herself the next.

[136]

A Momentous Interview

Not daring to think long about it lest she lose her determination, she started that very afternoon on her surprising errand.

She had the carriage to herself, for she had been to tea with a friend, and on her way home she asked the coachman to stop at a house in Carlton Terrace.

Reaching the house, Patty sent her card in by the footman, and awaited results with a beating heart.

The footman returned to the carriage door, saying, Sir Otho Markleham would be pleased to see Miss Fairfield, and resolutely crushing down her timidity, Patty went in.

She was ushered into a large and formal drawing-room, and waited there a few moments alone.

She wished she had been asked into a library, or some more cosy room, for the stiff hangings, and massive furniture were oppressive. But she had no time for further thought, for Sir Otho entered the room.

He bowed with exceeding courtesy, but with a surprised air, which was indeed only natural.

Frightened almost out of her wits, Patty extended her hand, and though she tried to conquer her embarrassment, her voice trembled, as she said: "How do you do, Sir Otho? I've come to see you."

She tried to speak jauntily, but there was a queer little break in her voice.

"So I perceive," said Sir Otho, coldly. "May I ask why I have this honour?"

This was too much for Patty. Her nerves were strained almost to the breaking point, and when Sir Otho spoke so repellently, she realised how foolish her little plan had been, and how hopeless was her dream of reconciling this dreadful old man and his daughter. Partly, then, because of her overwrought nerves, and partly because of the downfall of her cherished hopes, Patty burst into tears.

She rarely cried, almost never, unless at some injustice or undeserved unkindness. But when she did cry, it was done as she did everything else, with a whole-souled enthusiasm.

Utterly unable to control herself, for a few moments she sobbed, and shook in paroxysms of emotion.

The old gentleman fairly danced around.

"Bless my soul!" he exclaimed; "what *is* the matter? What does this mean? Did you come into my house for the purpose of having a fit of hysterics?"

A Momentous Interview

Now Patty wasn't a bit hysterical; it was merely a sudden blow of disappointment, and she would have been over it in a moment, but that Sir Otho made matters worse by storming at her.

"Stop it, do you hear? I won't have such goings on in my house! You are a madwoman!"

As Patty's sobs grew quieter, and she sat softly weeping into an already soaked handkerchief, her host's mood seemed to change also.

"When I consented to see Miss Patricia Fairfield," he said, quoting her name as it appeared on the card she had sent in, "I didn't know I was to be subjected to this extraordinary treatment."

"I d-didn't know it e-either," said Patty, wiping her eyes, and trying to smile. Then, as she saw Sir Otho's hard old face beginning to soften a little, she smiled at him through her tears.

"There, there, my dear, don't cry," he said, with a clumsy imitation of gentleness. "Shall I ring for a maid? Will you have some sal volatile?"

"No," said Patty, trying hard to check her sobs; "no, I will go away."

"But what's it all about?" said the bewildered old man. "What made you cry?"

"You did," said Patty, with such suddenness that he nearly fell over.

"I? Bless my soul! What did I do?"

"You were so c-cross," said Patty, weeping afresh at the remembrance of his cold looks.

"Well, never mind, child, I won't be cross again. Tell me all about it."

Surely Sir Otho was melting! Patty sagaciously believed he was touched by her tears, so made no desperate effort to stop them.

"I c-can't tell you now. You're not in a k-kind m-mood."

"Yes, I am; try to tell me, my dear child."

Patty thought she had never known any one who could turn from anger to kindness so suddenly, but she resolved to strike while the iron was hot.

"It's about K-Kitty," she said, still sobbing, but peeping out from behind her handkerchief to see how he took this broadside.

"I supposed so," he said, with a sigh. "Well, what about her?"

"She's your daughter, you know," went on Patty, growing more daring, as she slyly watched the old gentleman's expression.

A Momentous Interview

"Is she, indeed? I'd forgotten the fact."

This, though in a sarcastic tone, was better than his usual disavowal of the relationship.

"And did you stop in here, and treat me to this absurd scene, just to inform me concerning my family tree?"

"N-no," said Patty, resorting to tears again. "I stopped in, to—to ask you s-something."

"Well, out with it! Are you afraid of me?"

This nettled Patty.

"No;" she said, starting to her feet. Her tears had stopped now, and her eyes were blazing. "No! I am not afraid of you! I'm sorry I broke down. I was foolishly nervous. But I'm over it now. I came in here, Sir Otho Markleham, to ask you to make peace with your daughter, and to propose to you a pleasant way to do so. But you have been so cross and ugly, so sarcastic and cruel, that I see the utter hopelessness of trying to reconcile you two. I was foolish even to think of it! Lady Kitty is gentle and sweet in many ways, but she has inherited your obstinate, stubborn——"

"Pigheaded," suggested Sir Otho, politely.

"Yes! Pigheaded disposition, and though, as the older, you ought to make the advance,

you'll never do it—and she never will—and—
so——"

Patty broke down again, this time from sheer
sadness of heart at the irrevocable state of
things.

Her face buried in her handkerchief, to her
great surprise she felt a kindly touch on her
shoulder.

" Don't condemn me too soon, little one; and
don't condemn me unheard. Suppose I tell you
that some of my ideas have undergone a change
since Miss Yankee Doodle has taken it upon
herself to scold me."

" Oh! " said Patty, rendered almost breathless
with amazement at the kind tone and the gentle
touch.

" But suppose it's very hard for an old man
like me to uproot some feelings that have
grown and strengthened with the passing
years."

" But if they're bad and unworthy feelings,
you *want* to uproot them! " cried Patty.

" Yes," said Sir Otho, " I do. And though
my irascible and taciturn nature won't let me admit this to any one else, I'll confess to you, Miss
Yankee Doodle, I do want to pull them up, root
and branch."

A Momentous Interview

Sir Otho looked so brave and manly as he made this confession, which was truly difficult for him, that Patty grasped his hand in both hers, and cried: "Oh, what a *splendid* man you are! I'll *never* be afraid of you again!"

"You *weren't* afraid of me, child. That's why your words had weight with me. You fearlessly told me just what I was, and I had the grace to be ashamed of myself."

"Never mind that now," said Patty, eagerly. "Do you want to be friends again with Kitty?"

"More than anything on earth."

"Well, then, let me manage it; and do it the way I want you to, will you?"

Patty's voice and smile were very wheedlesome, and Sir Otho smiled in response, as he said:

"You've surely earned the right to manage it. How shall it be done? Will Kitty meet me halfway?"

"I think she will," said Patty, slowly. "But she's not very tractable, you know. Indeed, Sir Otho, she's such a contrary-minded person, that if she knew you wanted to be kind to her, she'd likely run away."

"Miss Patricia," said Sir Otho, gravely, "you can't tell me anything about my daughter

Catharine that I don't already know. And she is, indeed, contrary-minded, on occasion. As you so justly observed, she inherits my obstinate and cross-grained disposition."

" And yet she's so lovely to look at," sighed Patty.

" Ah, well, she didn't get her good looks from me, I'll admit."

" I think she did," said Patty, looking critically at the fine old face, with a thoughtful gaze that was very amusing.

" Well, are you going to detail to me the plan of this rather difficult campaign? "

" Yes, I am. And I hope you'll see it as I do."

" If I don't, I have little doubt but you can change my views. Will you have time to drink a cup of tea with me? We can plan so much more cosily over the teacups."

" Yes, I will," said Patty, consulting her watch.

" Then let us have it served in the library, and not in this depressing room, which you must associate with stormy outbursts of woe."

Patty laughed, and followed the stately old gentleman into the library, where tea was soon served.

A Momentous Interview

"One lump?" said Patty, holding the sugar-tongs poised over a teacup, while she put her head on one side and smiled at her host.

"Two, please. It's delightful to have some one make my tea for me, and you do it very prettily."

"But, alas!" said Patty, in mock despair, "I'll soon be supplanted here, by that 'obstinate, cross-grained' Lady Kitty."

"Why are you so sure she'll come back here to live?"

"Just give her the chance, and see," said Patty, wagging her head sagaciously, as she poured her own tea.

"How *much* pleasanter this is than squabbling," she observed, glancing happily at her host.

"Yes, or crying," said he, a bit teasingly, and Patty blushed.

"That's past history," she said; "and *now* I'll tell you my plan."

The details of the plan kept them both talking for some time, and then Patty had to hurry away to reach home at her appointed hour.

"Now, I won't see you again until then," she

said, as they parted at the door. "But I know you won't fail me."

"Not I!" said Sir Otho, and with his hand on his heart, he made a profound bow, and Patty drove homeward in the happiest mood she had known for many a day.

CHAPTER XI

THE BIRTHDAY PARTY

PATTY'S birthday party was a great success.

As a rule, young people love a " dress-up " party, and the guests all entered into the spirit of the thing.

Lady Hamilton was in her element.

For the occasion, she had engaged a large salon, and aside from the pretty floral decorations, there were dolls and Teddy Bears and rocking horses, and all sorts of children's toys and games. On the walls hung bright-colored prints, intended for nursery use, and little, low chairs and ottomans stood about.

Of course, Lady Hamilton, as hostess, did not dress like a child, but wore one of her own lovely, trailing white house-gowns.

When the guests arrived they were shown to dressing-rooms, where white-capped nurses awaited them, and assisted them to lay aside their wraps.

Then led to the salon by these same nurses,

the guests were presented to Lady Hamilton and Patty. Such shouts of laughter as arose at these presentations! The young people, dressed as tiny children, came in with a shy air (not always entirely assumed), and made funny little, bobbing curtseys. Some, finger in mouth, could find nothing to say; others of more fertile brain, babbled childishly, or lisped in baby-talk.

Before many had arrived, Patty and Lady Kitty were in such roars of laughter they could scarcely welcome the rest.

Tom Meredith was a dear. Though a boy nearly six feet tall, he had a round, cherubic face, and soft, curly hair. He wore a white dress of simple " Mother Hubbard " cut, the fulness hanging from a yoke, and ending just below his knees, in lace-edged frills. White stockings, and white kid pumps adorned his feet, and his short curls were tied at one side with an immense white bow. He was such a smiling, good-natured chap, and looked so girl-ish and sweet in his white frock, that Patty at once called him Baby Belle, and the name ex-actly suited him.

" Did you come all alone? " asked Lady Hamilton.

" Yeth, ma'am," replied Tom, rolling up his

eyes in pretended diffidence. " My nurthie
went to a ball game, tho I had to come all by
mythelf. But I'th a big dirl, now ! "

" You are indeed," said Patty, glancing at his
stalwart proportions, " but you're surely the
belle of this ball."

Grace Meredith was a little Dutch girl, and
was charming in the picturesque Holland head-
gear, and a tight-waisted, long-skirted blue
gown, that just cleared the tops of her clatter-
ing wooden sabots. She talked a Dutch dialect,
or rather, what she imagined was such, and if
not real Hollandese, it was at least, very amusing and funny.

Mabel Hartley looked very sweet as Little Red
Riding-Hood, and she carried a little basket on
her arm, which contained a real pat of butter.

Sinclair and Bob Hartley were the Princes in
the Tower, and the black velvet suits and white
lace collars were exceedingly becoming to them.
They wore wigs of long flaxen hair, and often
fell into the pose of the celebrated picture, to
the delight of all who saw them. But when not
posing as a tableau, they were so full of antics
that Patty told them they were more like Court
Jesters than Princes.

" Clowns, you mean," said Bob, as with a flash

of his black satin legs he leap-frogged over Sinclair's back.

" Behave yourselves, Princes! " admonished
Patty, and in a second, the two stood motionless,
side by side, as in the great painting.

" You certainly must be photographed like
that," exclaimed Lady Hamilton; and then a
brilliant idea came to her and she sent a message at once to a well-known photographer to
send one of his men and a camera at once.

And so, the regular programme of the party
was suspended while photographs of the guests
were taken. Singly and in groups they were
snapped off as fast as the camera could be ad-
justed, and Lady Hamilton promised to send
copies to their homes later.

Some of the young people had hired very
elaborate costumes and represented celebrated
works of art.

Gainsborough's " Blue Boy," and Velasquez'
" Maria Teresa," were truly beautiful, while
Van Dyck's " Baby Stuart," made a lovely picture. But equally interesting were the less pre-
tentious characters and costumes.

Simple Simon was a favourite with all. A
faded blue smock frock, and a battered old hat
formed his characteristic garb, and long,

straight yellow locks, and a stupid, open-mouthed expression of face made him look like the traditional Simon. He was a boy of much original wit, and his funny repartee proved him, in reality, far from simple-minded.

Little Miss Muffet was present, and Struwelpeter, and "Alice," and a merry brother and sister had to cut up many roguish antics before they were recognised as "The Heavenly Twins."

Mary, Mary, Quite Contrary, wore a pretty Dolly Varden costume, and carried a watering-pot, while Little Boy Blue shyly blew his horn at her. There were several Lord Fauntleroys, and Buster Browns and Rollos, and also a great many who represented nobody in particular, but just a dear little child.

Mr. Fairfield and Nan, though they had said they would come to the party dressed as children, had changed their minds, and arrived later than the others, wearing the garb of elderly people.

They said they were the grandparents, come to look at the children enjoy themselves.

Nan made a very sweet old lady, with white wig, and gold glasses, while Mr. Fairfield pretended to be an old man, cross and gouty. But

Patty's Friends

so funny was his ferocious crustiness that nobody felt in awe of him.

Led by Lady Hamilton, the boys and girls
played all sorts of merry children's games.

" Ring Around a Rosy," " London Bridge is
Falling Down," " Hide the Thimble," and
other such infantile entertainments proved exceedingly mirth-provoking. The big babies
were continually crying over fancied woes, and
sometimes even the historic characters grew
humorously quarrelsome.

At half-past four supper was served. The
children were formed in pairs for a grand
march. To the strains of " The Baby's Opera "
they marched to another room, where a long
table was set for them.

At each place was a bread-and-milk set, and a
mug which was lettered in gilt, " For a Good
Child."

The mugs were especially pretty ones, and
were to be taken home as souvenirs. At each
place was a bib with strings, and when these
were tied around their necks, the big " children " looked absurd indeed.

In keeping with their assumed rôles, their table
manners were not impeccable, and many fists
pounded on the table, while babyish voices

The Birthday Party

said: " Me wants me thupper," or " Div me some beddy-butter! " But though the bowls and mugs betokened infantile fare, the supper really served included dainty salads and sandwiches, followed by ices, jellies and cakes, and was fully enjoyed by the healthy appetites which belong to young people of eighteen or thereabouts.

After supper, they returned to the drawing-room for a dance.

Delightful music was played, and it was a pretty sight to see the fancy costumes gracefully flit about in the dance.

When it was nearly time to go home, one of the " nurses " came to Lady Hamilton saying that a belated guest had arrived.

" Who is it? " asked Lady Hamilton, surprised that any one should arrive so late.

" He says he is Peter Pan," answered the maid.

" Show him in, at once," said Lady Hamilton, " we surely want to see Peter Pan—the boy who never *could* grow up."

And then through the doorway came a figure that unmistakably represented Peter Pan.

The well-known costume of russet browns and autumn-leaf tints, the small, close cap with its single feather, and the fierce-looking dagger were all there. To be sure, it was a much *larger* Peter Pan than any of them had seen in the play, but otherwise it was surely Peter.

At first, Lady Hamilton looked completely bewildered, and then, as she realised that it was really her own father, she turned pale and then very pink.

Patty stood near her, and though she didn't know what might happen, she felt sure Lady Hamilton would be quite able to cope with the situation.

And so she was. After the first dazed moment, she stepped forward, and offering her hand, said cordially:

"Welcome, Peter Pan! We are indeed glad to see you. We're sorry you couldn't come earlier, but pray fall right into place with the rest of our little guests."

It was the nature of Sir Otho Markleham to do thoroughly whatever he did at all.

So, now, throwing himself into the spirit of the moment, he made friends with the young people at once. He entertained them with stories of his thrilling adventures with the pirates; he told them how he lost his shadow, he explained all about Fairies, and soon the other guests were all crowded about him, listening breathlessly to his talk.

Lady Hamilton, standing a little to one side of the listening group, looked at her father. She realised at once what it all meant. She knew that Patty had persuaded him to come, and that it meant complete reconciliation between father and daughter. The whole matter could be discussed later, if they chose, but the mere presence of her father beneath her roof meant forgiveness and peace between them.

Softly Patty came up beside her and clasped her hand. "You're a witch," whispered Lady Hamilton, as she warmly returned the pressure. "How did you ever accomplish this?"

"Never mind that, now," said Patty, her eyes shining. "Are you glad?"

"Glad! Yes, only that's a short word to express my joy and my gratitude to you. But you took a risk! Suppose I had fainted, or done something foolish in my great surprise."

"Oh, I knew you better than that," returned Patty. "Isn't he a dear in that Peter Pan suit? And, only think, he took off his beloved 'sideboards,' so he'd look the character better."

"They'll soon grow again," said Lady Hamil-

ton, carelessly; " but what I can't understand
is why he came at all."

" Because he loves you," whispered Patty,
" and you love him. And you've both been
acting like silly geese, but now that's all
over."

" Yes, it is! " And Lady Hamilton gave a
soft sigh of relief. Then, following her father's
example, she devoted herself to her young
guests, and the time passed pleasantly until their
departure.

Of course, these young people knew nothing of
the state of affairs between " Peter Pan " and
his hostess, though they soon discovered the
identity of Sir Otho.

Soon after six, the " children " went away, de-
claring that it had been the event of the season,
and they had never enjoyed a party more. The
three Fairfields took leave at the same time, and
Lady Hamilton was left alone with her father.

Exactly what was said in the next half hour
neither of them ever told, but when it was past,
the two were entirely reconciled, and Lady
Kitty had consented to return to her father's
house to live. Then she sent a note to the Fairfields, asking them all to dine with herself and
her father that evening.

The Birthday Party

"And meantime, Kitty," said Sir Otho, " I'll go and get out of this foolish toggery."

"Yes, but save that suit to be photographed in. I must have your picture to put with those of the other ' children.' "

Sir Otho went away, enveloped in a long raincoat, and promising to return at the dinner hour. It was a merry dinner party that night.

Patty had a new frock in honour of the occasion, and as she donned the pretty demitoilette of pale green gauze, Nan said it was the most becoming costume she had ever worn.

" Now that you're really eighteen, Patty," she said, " I think you might discard hair-ribbons."

" No, thank you," said Patty, as Louise tied her big, white bow for her. " I'll wear them a little longer. At least as long as I'm in this country where Dukes and Earls run wild. When I get back to New York, I'll see about it."

" Good-evening, Miss Yankee Doodle," said Sir Otho, as he met her again at dinner. " Once more the American has conquered the English, and I would be greatly honoured by your kind acceptance of this tiny memento of the occasion."

As Sir Otho spoke, he handed Patty a small

jeweller's box. She opened it and saw a dear little brooch in the form of an American flag. The Stars and Stripes were made of small sparkling brilliants of the three colours, and the twinkling effect was very beautiful.

" It is lovely! " she exclaimed; " how can I ever thank you! This is one of my very choicest birthday gifts, and I have received a great many."

" It is nothing," said Sir Otho, " compared to what you have given me," and he glanced affectionately toward his daughter.

And this was all he ever said by way of expressing his gratitude to Patty, but it was enough, for the deep tone of his voice, and the suggestion of tears in his eyes, proved his inexpressible appreciation of Patty's achievement.

Then the matter was dropped entirely, and the conversation became general and gay. Sir Otho proved to be as entertaining to older people as he had been to the children at the party, and Lady Kitty was in her most charming mood. Mr. and Mrs. Fairfield quite did their share toward the general entertainment, but Patty was queen of the feast. She enjoyed it all, for she dearly loved a festivity of any sort, but tonight she was specially happy to think that her plan had succeeded, and that she had given to her dear friend Kitty what she most wanted in all the world.

"And I trust it will not be long," said Sir Otho, " before you will all accept an invitation to dine with me in Carlton Terrace, with Lady Hamilton presiding at my table."

This invitation was delightedly accepted, and then they all went up to the Fairfields' drawing-room, and Patty sang songs, and they all sang choruses, and then, as a final surprise, came a great, beautiful birthday cake, with eighteen lighted candles.

Then Patty cut the cake, and there were more congratulations and good wishes all round, and for pretty nearly the eighteenth time in her life Patty declared it was the best birthday she had ever had.

CHAPTER XII

SUMMER PLANS

"AS usual," said Mr. Fairfield, smiling, "the question is, what is to be done with Patty?"

"Yes," agreed Patty, complacently, "you and Nan are usually trying to dispose of me in some way. It's lucky I'm good-natured and don't mind being left behind."

"That's a pretty speech!" exclaimed Nan, "after we've begged and coaxed you to go with us!"

"So you have, my pretty little Stepmother— so you have; and I'm just ungrateful enough not to want to go."

It was about a week after the birthday party, and the Fairfields were making their plans for the summer. The elders wanted to travel in Switzerland and Germany. Patty did not want to go with them, but her dilemma was, which of several delightful invitations to accept.

"You see," she went on, "I'm invited to spend June in five separate places, each one lovelier than the other. Now I can't chop myself up into five pieces."

"You can chop June up into five pieces," suggested Nan.

"Yes, but if I go to a country house to make a good long visit, I want to stay about a month. A week here and then a week there is so unsatisfactory. However, after much thoughtful brooding over the question, I've cut out three, and that brings my quandary down to only two places to decide between."

"Lady Hamilton's being one," observed her father.

"Yes, Kitty's is one; and Mabel Hartley's is the other. Of course, if I spend June with Kitty, we'll be right here in London all the time, and though I love it, yet I love the country too. Now, if I go to Mabel's, I'll have a beautiful experience of real English country life."

"You would enjoy it, I'm sure," said Nan; "and I think you'd better decide to go to Cromarty Manor, and then, if for any reason, you don't like it, come back, and put in the rest of your time with Lady Kitty."

"Nan, that's an inspiration!" cried Patty, running across the room, and clasping Nan in one of her rather strenuous embraces.

Patty's Friends

"Look out! You'll break her!" cried Mr. Fairfield, in great pretence of fear.

"No, indeed!" said Patty, "she's too substantial. And anyway, such a clever suggestion deserves ample recognition."

Patty sat on the arm of Nan's chair, and amused herself by twisting Nan's curly hair into tight little spirals.

"Stop that, Patty," said her father; "you make Nan look like a pickaninny."

"No matter what she looks like, if it's becoming," said Patty, serenely. "But truly, Nan, you ought to wear your hair like that; it's awfully effective!"

The spirals now stood out all round Nan's face, like a spiky frame, but the good-natured victim only laughed, as she said, "Never mind me, let's get these great questions settled."

So, after some more talk and discussion, it was settled that Patty should accept the Hartleys' urgent invitation to Cromarty Manor, for, at least, a part of June, and then, if she cared to, stay also a time with Lady Hamilton.

"It may sound silly," said Patty, thoughtfully, "but I can't help feeling that Mabel not only wants me to visit her this summer, but she needs me. Now, I don't mean to be conceited, but, don't you know, you can tell when people seem to need you, if only in a trivial way."

"I understand," said Nan, quickly; "and you're not conceited a bit, Patty. Mabel does need you. She is a sweet girl, but sometimes she seems to me the least bit morbid; no, not quite that, but verging that way. She adores you, and I'm perfectly sure that your companionship will do her a world of good."

"I hope so," said Patty; "I love Mabel, but there is something about her I can't quite understand."

"You'll probably find out what it is, when you're staying with her," said her father, "and I know, Patty, you'll do all in your power to brighten her up. The Merediths live near them, don't they?"

"Yes; only a mile or two away. And the Merediths are gay enough for anybody. If they're at home this summer, there'll be plenty of fun going on, I'm sure."

"Lady Hamilton will miss you a lot," said Nan; "what does she say to your going?"

"Oh, she says she'll miss me," said Patty, "and so she will, some, but it's not like it was when she was here, alone. Now that she's settled in her father's house again, she has so much to occupy her time and attention she's never lonely. Of course, she's just as fond of me, and I am of her, but since she's gone away from here, I don't see so much of her. And, truly, she doesn't need me, and Mabel does. So I'll go to Mabel's first, and I shouldn't be surprised if I stay there until you people come back from your trip. Mrs. Hartley asked me for the whole summer, you know, but you won't be gone more than a month or six weeks, will you?"

"Not more than two months," answered her father, " and you know, chickabiddy, if ever you want to join us, I'll send for you, or come for you myself, whenever you say the word. Just telegraph me, and I'll respond at once."

"All right; I will if I want to. But there's too much fun for me in civilization to want to go wandering off to the ends of the earth."

"And you may decide to go to Herenden Hall for a time."

"Yes, I may. I'd love to visit Lady Herenden again, if I thought that Earl gentleman wouldn't be there."

"He probably won't be," said Nan. "I daresay you scared him away from there forever."

"Even so, I didn't scare him as much as he scared me," returned Patty, "but I do hope there won't be any Earls at Cromarty. I like plain, big boys better."

"Those Hartley boys are fine fellows," observed Mr. Fairfield. "Young Meredith has more fun and jollity, but the Hartleys are of a sterling good sort. I like the whole family, and I'm glad, Patty girl, that you've decided to go there. I'll willingly leave you in Mrs. Hartley's care, and I'm sure you'll have a good time."

"Of course I shall, Daddy, and I'll write you every day, if you want me to."

"Not quite so often, my dear. Twice a week, will be all you'll find time for, I'm certain."

"Quite likely," said Patty, who was not very fond of writing letters.

Only a week later, Patty was to go away with the Hartleys. And a week was not a very long time for her preparations. There was shopping to do, and calling, and, as Nan and Mr. Fairfield were leaving at the same time, they were to give up their hotel apartment for the present.

But Lady Hamilton insisted that Patty must look upon Sir Otho's big house in Carlton Terrace as her own home. If she cared to run up to London for a few days at any time, she would be more than welcome at Lady Kitty's. Or she could leave there any trunks or other belongings that she wished. This greatly pleased Mr. Fairfield, for he felt more comfortable at leaving Patty, to know that she had a foothold in London, and somebody to look after her, should she care to leave Cromarty before her parents' return.

At last the day of departure came, and Mr. Fairfield accompanied Patty to the station to meet the Hartleys for the journey.

It was with a homesick heart that Patty bade her father good-bye. Somehow, she suddenly felt that she was leaving her own people to go away with strangers. But she knew she must not be foolish, so she bravely kept back the tears and said good-bye with a tender, if not a gay, smile.

"It is the loveliest thing," said Mabel, after they were settled in the train, "to think that you're really going with us. I wanted you to, so dreadfully, but I didn't urge it very much, for fear you wouldn't enjoy yourself with us."

"I always enjoy myself," said Patty, "but I know I shall be happy with you."

Summer Plans

"We'll try to make you so, Miss Fairfield," said Bob, earnestly, and Patty smiled at him, and said:

"Then the first thing you can do toward it, is to drop that formal name, and call me Patty. I'm not really grown-up enough for the other."

"No, I don't think you are," said Bob, as he looked at her critically. "So, as we're all to live under one roof for a time, we'll be first namers all round."

"Good!" said Sinclair, "that suits me; and now, Mater, when you're ready, we'll go in to luncheon.

Patty thought luncheon in the dining car was great fun. Only four could sit at a table, but as Mrs. Hartley had a slight headache and did not care to talk, she and Grandma Cromarty sat at another table, and left the four young people to chatter by themselves.

Everything interested Patty, from the unusual things she found on the menu to the strange sights she saw from the window.

This was her first trip in this direction, for they were travelling toward Leicester, and the scenes were all new to her.

The boys were full of fun and nonsense, and Mabel was so gay and jolly that Patty began to think she had imagined the girl was of a sad nature. They all told funny stories, and made absurd jokes, and poked fun at each other, and Patty concluded she was likely to have a very jolly summer with the Hartleys. Back they went after luncheon to their funny parlour car, which had double seats facing each other, with a small table between.

" Just the place for a game," said Sinclair, as the four took their seats, two on either side of the table.

" What sort of a game? " asked Patty.

" Oh, I don't know; I'll make one up." The boy took a bit of chalk from his pocket, and marked off the table into various sections, with a circle in each corner, and crosses here and there.

" Now," he explained, as he offered each player a coin, " this isn't money, you know. They're merely counters, for the time being. But when the game is over you must all give them back to me, because they'll be money again then."

" But what do we do with them? " asked Patty, who was greatly interested in any game.

" I'll show you. These places are homes, and these are wilderness. If you're in the wilderness you may be captured, but if you're at home, you can't be."

The game was really a mix-up of parcheesi, halma, and some others; to which were added some original rules out of Sinclair's own head. Patty and Bob were partners against the other two, and soon the quartette were deeply absorbed in the game.

" You are the cleverest boy, to make this up ! " cried Patty, as her side won, and they prepared to begin over again.

" Oh, he often makes up games," said Mabel. " We all do, only Sinclair's are always the best."

" Mine are very good, though," observed Bob, modestly.

" Good enough, yes," said Sinclair; " only usually they're so difficult that nobody can win but yourself."

Bob made a profound bow at this compliment, and then the game went on. It seemed impossible that they had been about five hours on the train, when it was time to get out. They had reached Leicester, and from there were to drive to Cromarty Manor.

Two vehicles met them at the station.

Into one of these, a comfortable victoria, Sinclair assisted the four ladies, and in the other, the boys rode up with the luggage. The drive was beautiful, and Patty warmly expressed her gratitude to Mrs. Hartley, for inviting her to this delightful experience of English country life.

" It *is* beautiful," said Mrs. Hartley, looking about her. " I'm always glad to get back from London to the restful quiet of these great trees and the far-away, peaceful hills."

Mabel's mood had changed. She no longer laughed and jested, and though sweet and gentle as ever, the hint of sadness had again crept into her face, and her speech was slow and quiet. Patty adapted her mood to the other's, and it was almost in silence they drove along the country roads.

It was a long ride, and it was nearly dusk when at last they arrived at Cromarty Manor.

An old servant came out from the Porter's Lodge to open the high iron gates for them.

He gave them a warm greeting, which seemed a heart-felt welcome, and not merely the speech of a paid dependant, and then they drove on toward the house.

The whole effect was so beautiful that it almost took Patty's breath away. It was not a bit like Herenden Hall, it was more like an old feudal castle. The picturesque house was of gray stone, with towers and turrets almost entirely covered with ivy. From the ivy the birds flew in and out, and the darkness of the surrounding trees and tall shrubbery gave the place a weird and fairly mysterious appearance.

"You feel the charm of it, don't you?" said Mrs. Hartley, kindly, as she looked at Patty's rapt face and serious eyes.

"Yes, indeed," said Patty, softly; "I can't explain it, but it casts a spell over me. Oh, I don't wonder you love it!"

But the darkness of the outer world was soon dispelled by a broad gleam of light, as the great front doors were thrown open. An old, gray-haired butler stood on the threshold, and greeted them with rather pompous respect and punctilious deference. The interior was quite in keeping with the outside view of the house. But though the old carved rafters and wainscoting were dark and heavy, cheerful lamps were in abundance, and in the halls and drawing-rooms, wax candles were lighted also.

At the first view on entering there seemed to be an interminable vista of rooms, that opened one from another; this was partly the effect of

[171]

the elaborate old architecture, and partly because of many long mirrors in various positions.

The furniture, tapestries and ornaments were
all of an epoch two centuries back, and the
whole picture fascinated Patty beyond all words.

"It's a wonderful place," she said at last;
"and after a week or two, I'm going to examine
it in detail. But at first I shall be satisfied just
to bask in its atmosphere."

"You'll do!" cried Bob, who had just arrived.
"If you hadn't appreciated Cromarty, we were
going to pack you straight back to London; but
you've acquitted yourself nobly. Nobody could
make a better speech than you did, and I'll
wager you didn't learn it beforehand either."

"I couldn't," said Patty, "because I didn't
know what the place was like. What few re-
marks you made about it seem like nothing,
now that I've begun to see it for myself."

"Yes, and you've only begun," said Sinclair.
"To-morrow, when you get further into the
heart of it, you'll surrender to its charm as
we all do."

"I'm sure I shall," agreed Patty, "and, indeed, I think I have already done so."

CHAPTER XIII

CROMARTY MANOR

L IFE at Cromarty Manor was very pleasant indeed.

Although Patty had not definitely realised it, she was thoroughly tired out by her London gaieties, and the peaceful quiet of the country brought her a rest that she truly needed.

Also, the Hartleys were a delightful family to visit. There is quite as much hospitality in knowing when to leave guests to themselves as there is in continually entertaining them.

And while the Hartleys planned many pleasures for Patty, yet there were also hours in the morning or early afternoon, when she was free to follow her own sweet will.

Sometimes she would roam around the historic old house, pausing here and there in some of the silent, unused rooms, to imagine romances of days gone by.

Sometimes she would stroll out-of-doors, through the orchards and woods, by ravines and

[173]

brooks, always discovering some new and beautiful vista or bit of scenery.

And often she would spend a morning, lying in a hammock beneath the old trees, reading a book, or merely day-dreaming, as she watched the sunlight play hide-and-seek among the leaves above her head.

One morning, after she had been at Cromarty Manor for about a week, Patty betook herself to her favourite hammock, carrying with her a book of Fairy Tales, for which she had never outgrown her childish fondness.

But the book remained unopened, for Patty's mind was full of busy thoughts.

She looked around at the beautiful landscape which, as far as the eye could reach included only the land belonging to the Cromarty estate. There were more than a thousand acres in all, much of which was cultivated ground, and the rest woodland or rolling meadows. Patty looked at the dark woods in the distance; the orchards nearer by; and, in her immediate vicinity, the beautiful gardens and terraces.

The latter, of which there were two, known as the Upper and Lower Terrace, were two hundred feet long and were separated by a sloping bank of green lawn, dotted with round flower beds.

Above the terraces rose the old house itself. The Manor was built of a grayish stone, and was of Elizabethan architecture.

More than two hundred years old, it had been remodelled and added to by its various successive owners, but much of its fine old, original plan was left.

Ivy clung to its walls, and birds fluttered in and out continually.

There was a tower on either side the great entrance, and Patty loved to fancy that awful and mysterious deeds had been committed within those frowning walls.

But there was no legend or tradition attached to the mansion, and all its history seemed to be peaceful and pleasant.

Even the quaint old yew-tree walk, with its strangely misshapen shrubbery, was bright and cheerful in the morning sunlight, and the lake rippled like silver, and gave no hint of dark or gloomy depths.

And yet, Patty couldn't help feeling that there was some shadow hanging over the Hartley family. They were never sad or low-spirited, but sometimes Mrs. Hartley would sigh, or

Patty's Friends

Grandma Cromarty would look anxious, as if at some unrelievable sorrow.

The boys were always light-hearted and gay, but Mabel often had moods of despondency, which, while they never made her cross or irritable, were so pathetic that it worried Patty's loving heart.

And so she lay in her hammock, gazing at the beauty all about her, and wondering what was the secret grief that harassed her dear friends. It never occurred to her that it was none of her affair, for Patty was possessed of a healthy curiosity, and moreover she was innately of a helpful nature, and longed to know what the trouble was, in a vague hope that she might be of some assistance.

" I know they're not rich," she said to herself, " for the whole place shows neglect and shabbiness; but there's something besides lack of money that makes Madam Cromarty sad."

The place was indeed in a state of unrepair. Though there were many servants, there were not enough to do all that should have been done. The two gardeners did their best to keep the flowers in order, but the elaborate conventional gardens, laid out in geometric designs, and intricate paths, called for a complete staff of trained workers, and in the absence of these, became overgrown at their borders and untidy in appearance.

It was the same indoors. The handsome old furniture, covered with silk brocades and tapestries, was worn and sometimes ragged in appearance. Some of the decorations showed need of regilding, and though the magnificent old carved woodwork, and tesselated floors could not be marred by time, yet many of the lesser appointments called for renovation or renewal. The Great Hall, as it was called, had best withstood the ravages of time, as it was wainscoted and ceiled in massive old oak.

It was a noble apartment, with recessed windows and panelled walls, and across one end was a raised platform from the back of which rose a wonderfully carved chimneypiece.

This apartment, in the palmier days of the Manor House, had been the Banqueting Hall, but as there was a smaller and more appropriate dining-room, the Hartleys used the Great Hall as a living room, and had gathered in it their dearest treasures and belongings. Grandma Cromarty had her own corner, with her knitting basket. In another corner was a

grand piano, and many other musical instruments. In one north bay window was Mabel's
painting outfit, and so large was the recess that
it formed a good-sized studio. On the walls,
hobnobbing with the ancient antlers and deers'
heads, trophies of the chase, were the boys' ten-
nis rackets, and in the outstretched arm of a
tall figure in armour, a lot of golfsticks rested
against the quartered shield.

"I suppose," Mabel had said, when they first
showed this room to Patty, " a great many
people would consider it desecration to fill up
this fine old place with all our modern stuff.
But we're modern, and so we make the carving
and tapestries give way to us."

" They like it," Patty had replied. " They
feel sorry for other houses where the carvings
and tapestries have to stay back in their own
old times. Now hear these old rafters ring to
modern music," and seating herself at the piano,
Patty began some rollicking songs that were of
decidedly later date than the old rafters.

Opening from the old Banqueting Hall was
the library. This had been left just as it was,
and the shelves full of old books were a never-
failing delight to Patty's browsing nature. A
gallery ran round all four sides, which was

reached by spiral iron staircases, and the deep-seated windows, with their old leather cushions, made delightful nooks in which to pore over the old volumes. There were many unused rooms in the Manor House. Many unexpected alcoves and corridors, and in these the old furniture was worn and decayed. The rooms that were lived in were kept in comfortable order, but Patty knew, had there been more house-servants, these other apartments would have been thrown open to light and air.

Surely, Patty decided, the Hartleys were pinched for money, but just as surely, she thought, that could not have the effect of casting that indefinite gloom over them which was now and then observable. And as she idly swung in her hammock, she made up her mind to ask about it.

" If they don't want to tell me, they needn't," she said to herself, " but they surely know me well enough now to know that I'm honestly interested in their life, and not merely trying to pry into their secrets."

But she could not quite decide which one of the family to ask about it. She would have preferred to ask Grandma Cromarty, but the old lady had a certain reserve, which, at times was forbidding, and Patty stood a little in awe of her.

Mrs. Hartley was kindly and responsive, but Patty rarely saw her except when the whole family was present. In the morning Mrs. Hartley was busy with household duties, and afternoons Patty and Mabel were usually together. Patty felt sure she could never ask Mabel, for though the two girls were confidential friends, there was a sensitiveness in Mabel's disposition that made Patty shrink from touching on what she felt might be a painful subject. Then there were the boys. Bob, at home on his vacation from college was Patty's chum and merry comrade, but she imagined he would cleverly evade a serious question. He was always chaffing, and while Patty was always glad to meet him on this ground, she almost knew he wouldn't talk seriously on family subjects. This left only Sinclair. Patty really liked Sinclair Hartley. A young man of about twenty, he was studying law in a nearby town, where he went every morning, returning in mid-afternoon.

He was kindly and courteous, and though often grave, was always appreciative of a joke, and quite ready to join in any fun. But he had a serious side, and Patty had enjoyed many long talks with him on subjects that never would interest Mabel or Bob.

And so she concluded that at the first opportunity, she would ask Sinclair what was the nature of the mystery that seemed to hang over the House of Hartley.

" Ah, there, Pitty-Pat! " called a gay voice, and looking around, Patty saw Bob strolling toward her across the lawn. " Want to go out on the lake and fish for pond-lilies? "

" Yes, indeed," said Patty, twisting herself out of the hammock. " What are you going to do with them? "

" Oh, just for the lunch table. Mabel's so everlastingly fond of them, you know."

Patty thought it was nice of Bob to remember his sister's tastes, and she willingly went with him toward the lake.

" How beautiful it all is! " she said as they went down the terrace steps and along the lake path which led through a pergola and around a curved corner called " The Alcove."

This delightful nook was a small open court of marble, adorned with pillars and statues, and partly surrounding a fountain.

" Yes, isn't it? " exclaimed Bob, enthusiastically. "You know, Patty, this old place is my joy and my despair. I love every stick and stone of it, but I wish we could keep it up in decent order. Heigh-ho! Just wait until I'm out of college. I'll do something then to turn an honest shilling, and every penny of it shall go to fix up the dear old place."

"What are you going to be, Bob?"

"An engineer. There's more chance for a fellow in that than in any other profession. Old Sinclair's for being a lawyer, and he'll be a good one, too, but it's slow work."

"You ought to go to America, Bob, if you want to get rich."

"I would, like a shot, if I could take the old house with me. But I'm afraid it's too big to uproot."

"I'm afraid it is. I suppose you wouldn't like to live in a brown-stone front on Fifth Avenue?"

"Never having seen your brown-stone Avenue, ma'am, I can't say; but I suppose a deer park and lake and several thousand acres of meadow land are not included with each house."

"No; not unless you take the whole of Manhattan Island."

"Even that wouldn't do; unless I had taken

it a few hundred years ago, and started the trees growing then."

"No, America wouldn't suit you," said Patty, thoughtfully, "any more than English country life would suit most of our American boys."

"But you like this life of ours?"

"I love it; for a time. And just now I am enjoying it immensely. Oh, what gorgeous lilies!"

They had reached the lake, and the quiet, well-behaved water was placidly rippling against the stone coping.

Bob untied the boat.

"It's an old thing," he said, regretfully; "but it's water-tight, so don't be afraid."

Patty went down the broad marble steps, and seated herself in the stern of the boat, while Bob took the rowing seat.

A few of his strong pulls, and they were out among the lily pads.

"Row around a bit before we gather them," suggested Patty, and Bob with long, slow strokes sent the boat softly and steadily along.

"Isn't it perfect?" said Patty, dreamily. "It seems as if nothing could stir me up on a day like this."

"Is that so?" said Bob, and with mischief in

his eyes, he began to rock the boat from side to side.

"You villain!" cried Patty, rudely stirred from her calm enjoyment; "take that!"

She dashed light sprays of water at him from over the side of the boat, and he returned by cleverly sprinkling a few drops on her from the blade of his oar.

"Why did you want to kick up a bobbery, when everything was so nice and peaceful?" she said, reproachfully.

"I shall always kick up a bobbery," he returned, calmly, "when you put on that romantic, sentimental air."

"I didn't put on any sentimental air! I was just enjoying the dreamy spirit of the lake."

"Thank you! That's the same as saying my society makes you sleepy."

"Nothing of the sort. And anyway, the dreamy mood has passed."

"Yes, I intended it should. Now, let's sing."

"All right; what?"

"The 'Little Kibosh,' I think. That's a good song to row by."

The young people at Cromarty Manor had already composed several songs which seemed to them choicest gems of musical composition.

Cromarty Manor

As a rule Patty and Bob made up the words, while Mabel and Sinclair arranged the tunes.

Sometimes the airs were adapted from well-known songs, and sometimes they were entirely original.

" The Little Kibosh " was one of their favourite nonsense songs, and now Patty and Bob sang it in unison as they rowed slowly about on the lake.

" It was ever so many years ago,
   On a prairie by the sea;
A little Kibosh I used to know
   By the name of Hoppity Lee.
His hair was as green as the driven snow,
   And his cheeks were as blue as tea.

" 'Twas just about night, or nearly noon
   When Hoppity Lee and I
Decided to go for a sail to the moon,
   At least, as far as the sky.
But instead of taking the Big Balloon,
   We sailed in a pumpkin pie.

" Dear little Hoppity Lee and I
   Were happy and glad and gay;
But the Dog Star came out as we passed by,
   And began to bark and bay.

Patty's Friends

And the little Kibosh fell out of the pie,
And into the Milky Way!

" I fished and fished for a year and a week
For dear little Hoppity Lee;
And at last I heard a small faint squeak
From the place where he used to be;
And he said, ' Go home, and never more seek,
Oh, never more seek for me ! ' "

CHAPTER XIV

UNCLE MARMADUKE

THAT very same evening Patty had a chance to speak to Sinclair alone.

It was just after dinner, and the lovely English twilight was beginning to cast long, soft shadows of the tall cypresses across the lawn. The various members of the family were standing about on the terrace, when Sinclair said, " You need some exercise, Patty; let's walk as far as the alcove."

Patty assented, and the two strolled away, while Mabel called after them, " Don't be gone long, for we're all going to play games this evening."

They all loved games, so Patty promised to return very soon.

" I never saw anything like this alcove before in my life," said Patty, as they reached the picturesque spot and sat down upon the curving marble seat.

" They are often found in the gardens of old English homes. Any arched or covered seat out of doors is called an alcove. But this is rather an elaborate one. The marble pillars are of fine design, and the whole thing is beautifully proportioned."

" Is it very old? "

" Yes, older than the house. You know the Cromartys have lived on this estate for several hundred years. But the original house was destroyed by fire, or nearly so, and the present house was built on the old foundations about the middle of the seventeenth century. If you're interested in these things, there are lots of books in the library, telling all about the history of the place."

" Indeed I am interested, and I shall look up the books, if you'll tell me what they are. Is there any legend or tradition connected with the place? "

" No. We have no ghosts at Cromarty Manor. We've always been a peaceful sort, except that my great uncle quarrelled with my grandfather."

" Mrs. Cromarty's husband? "

" Yes. He was Roger Cromarty—grandfather was, I mean—and he had a brother Marmaduke. They were both high-tempered, and Marmaduke after an unusually fierce quarrel left home and went to India. But have you never heard the story of the Cromarty Fortune?"

"No, I never have. Is it a sad story? Would you rather not tell me?"

"Why, no; it isn't a sad story, except that the conditions are rather sad for us. But there's no reason in the world why you shouldn't hear it, if you care to. Indeed, I supposed Mabel had already told it you."

"No, she never did. Will you?"

"Yes. But not here. Let us go in, and get the family all together, and we'll give you a dramatic recital of the Great Cromarty Mystery."

"Oh, is it a mystery story? How delightful. I love a mystery."

"I'm glad you do, but I assure you I wish it wasn't a mystery."

"Will it never be solved?"

"I fear not, now. But let us go back to the house, and tell the tale as it should be told."

They found that the others had already gone into the house, and were gathered round the big table that stood in the middle of the living room. As they joined the group, Sinclair said:

"Before we play games this evening, we are

going to tell Patty the story of Uncle Marmaduke's money."

Patty was surprised to note the different ex-
pressions on her friends' faces. Mabel seemed
to shrink into herself, as if in embarrassment or
sensitiveness. Mrs. Cromarty looked calmly
proud, and Mrs. Hartley smiled a little.

But Bob laughed outright, and said:

"Good! I'll help; we'll all help, and we'll
touch up the tale until it has all the dramatic
effect of a three-volume novel."

"It won't need touching up," said Sinclair.
"Just the plain truth is story enough of itself."

"You begin it, Grandy," said Bob, "and then,
when your imagination gives out, I'll take a
hand at it."

The old lady smiled.

"It needs no imagination, Robert," she said;
"if Patty cares to hear of our family misfortune, I'm quite willing to relate the tale."

"Oh, I didn't know it was a misfortune," cried
Patty. "I thought it was a mystery story."

"It's both," said Mrs. Cromarty, "but if the
mystery could be solved, it would be no misfortune."

"That sounds like an enigma," observed
Patty.

Uncle Marmaduke

"It's all an enigma," said Bob. "Go ahead, Grandy."

"The story begins," said Mrs. Cromarty, "with my marriage to Roger Cromarty. I was wed in the year 1855. My husband and I were happy during the first few years of our married life. He was the owner of this beautiful place, which had been in his family for many generations. My daughter, Emmeline, was born here, and when she was a child she filled the old house with her happy laughter and chatter. My husband had a brother, Marmaduke, with whom he was not on good terms. Before my marriage, this brother had left home, and gone to India. My husband held no communication with him, but we sometimes heard indirectly from him, and reports always said that he was amassing great wealth in some Indian commerce."

"Is that his portrait?" asked Patty, indicating a painting of a fine-looking man in the prime of life.

"Yes," said Mrs. Cromarty. "But the picture represents him as looking amiable, whereas he was always cross, grumpy, and irritable."

"Like me," commented Bob.

"No," said his mother, " I'm thankful to say that none of you children show the slightest

signs of Uncle Marmaduke's disposition. I was
only fifteen years old when he died, but I shall
never forget his scowling face and angry tones."

"Was he always cross?" asked Patty, amazed
that any one could be invariably ill-tempered.

"Always," said Mrs. Cromarty. "At least,
whenever he was here. I never saw him elsewhere."

"Go back, Grandy; you're getting ahead of
your story."

"Well, I tried my best to bring about a
reconciliation between the two brothers, but both
were proud and a bit stubborn. I could not
persuade my husband to write to Marmaduke,
and though I wrote to him myself, my letters
were torn up, and the scraps returned to me."

"Lovely old gentleman!" commented Bob.
"I'm glad my manners are at least better than
that!"

"At last, my husband, Mr. Roger Cromarty,
became very ill. I knew he could not recover,
and wrote Marmaduke to that effect. To my
surprise, I received a grim, but fairly polite
letter, saying that he would leave India at once,
and hoped to reach his brother's bedside in time
for a reconciliation."

"And did he?" asked Patty, breathlessly.

Uncle Marmaduke

"Yes, but that was all. My husband was dying when his brother came. They made peace, however, and arranged some business matters."

"Oh," cried Patty, "how glad you must have been that he did not come too late. What a comfort all these years, to know that they did make up their quarrel."

"Yes, indeed," assented Mrs. Cromarty. "But I have talked all I can. Emmeline, you may take up the narrative."

"I'll tell a little," said Mrs. Hartley, smiling; "but I shall soon let Sinclair continue. We all know this tale by heart, but only Sinclair can do full justice to the mysterious part of it. I was only ten years old when my father died, and Uncle Marmaduke came here to live. It changed the whole world for me. Where before all had been happiness and love, now all was unkindness and fear. None of us dared cross Uncle Marmaduke, for his fiery anger was something not to be endured. And beside being bad-tempered, he was erratic. He did most peculiar things, without any reason in them whatever. Altogether, he was a most difficult man to live with. But at my father's death he owned this estate, and we had to live with him or go homeless. He had plenty

of money, and he repaired and restored much
about the place. But even in this he was erratic. He would have masons in to renew the
crumbling plaster and brickwork in the cellars,
while the drawing-room furniture could go ragged and forlorn. He spent his money freely
for anything he wanted himself, but was nig-
gardly toward mother and myself. However,
he always told us that at his death we should
inherit his wealth. The estate, also, he willed
to mother. He lived with us for about five
years, and then was killed by a fall from his
horse. I was a girl of fifteen then, and when
he was brought in, mangled and almost dead,
he called for me. I went to his bedside, trembling, for even then I feared he was going to
scold me. But he could only speak in hesitating,
disjointed sentences. It was with difficulty I
gathered that he was trying to give me some information about his fortune. I wish now I had
tried to help him tell me; but at that time it
seemed heartless to think of such things when
the poor man was dying, and I soothed him, and
begged him not to try to talk, when it was such
an exertion."

"Oh, Mother," wailed Bob, "if you'd only
listened, instead of talking yourself!"

Mrs. Hartley smiled, as if she were used to such comments at this part of the story.

" Well," she said, " I think Sinclair may take up the recital here. That is, if you're interested, Patty? "

" If I'm interested! Indeed I am! It's very exciting, and I want it all now; no ' continued in our next.' "

" We don't know the end, ourselves," said Mabel, with such a wistful look in her eyes that Patty went over and sat by her, and with her arm round her listened to the rest of the story.

" Well, then," said Sinclair, in his grave, kindly voice, " Uncle Marmaduke tried very hard to communicate to mother and Grandy something about his fortune. But his accident had somehow paralysed his throat, and he could scarcely articulate. But for an hour or more, as he lay dying, he would look at them with piercing glances, and say what sounded like dickens! gold! "

" Did he mean gold money? " asked Patty, impulsively.

" They didn't know, then. But they thought at the time that dickens! was one of his angry expletives, as he was given to such language. The gold, they felt sure, referred to his fortune, which he had always declared he would leave to Grandmother. Then he died, without being able to say any other except those two words, gold and dickens."

" He might have meant Charles Dickens," suggested Patty, who dearly loved to guess at a puzzle.

"As it turned out, he did," said Sinclair, serenely; " but that's ahead of the story."

" And, too," said Mrs. Hartley, " the way in which he finally articulated the word, by a great effort, and after many attempts, was so—so explosive, that it sounded like an ejaculation far more than like a noted author."

" Years went by," continued Sinclair, " and Grandy and mother were left with the old Cromarty estate, and nothing to keep it up with."

" We had a small income, my boy," said his grandmother.

" Yes, but not enough to keep the place as it should be kept. However, no trace could be found of Uncle Marmaduke's money. He was generally supposed to have brought a large fortune home from India, but it seemed to have vanished into thin air. His private papers and belongings showed no records of stocks or bonds, no bank books, and save for a small amount of ready money he had by him, he seemed to be penniless. Of course, he wasn't; the way he had lived, and the money he had spent indicated that he had a fortune somewhere; and, too, there was his promise to leave it to Grandy. Of course, the conclusion was that he had hidden this fortune."

"A hidden fortune!" exclaimed Patty, blissfully. "Oh, what a lovely mystery! Why, you couldn't have a better one!"

"I think a discovered fortune would be far better," said Mabel, and Patty clasped her friend's hand in sympathy.

"At last," said Sinclair, "a *very* bright lawyer had a glimmering of an idea that Uncle Marmaduke's last words had some meaning to them. He inquired of the ladies of the house, and learned that the late Mr. Marmaduke had been exceedingly fond of reading Dickens, and that he was greatly attached to his own well-worn set of the great author's works. 'Ah, ha!' said the *very* bright lawyer. 'Between those well-thumbed pages, we will find many Bank of England notes, or certificates of valuable stocks!' They flew to the library, and thoroughly searched all the volumes of the set. And what do you think they found?"

Patty's Friends

"Nothing," said Patty, wagging her head solemnly.

"Exactly that! Save for a book-marker here and there, the volumes held nothing but their own immortal stories. 'Foiled again!' hissed the *very* bright lawyer. But he kept right on being foiled, and still no hoard of securities was found."

"But what about the gold?" said Patty. "They didn't expect to find gold coins in Dickens' books?"

"No, but they fondly hoped they'd find a mysterious paper in cryptogram, like the 'Gold Bug,' you know, telling them to go out in the dark of the moon, and dig north by northwest under the old apple tree."

"Don't try to be funny, Clair," put in Bob; "go on with the yarn. You're telling it well to-night."

"And then," said Sinclair, looking from one to another of his interested hearers, "and then the years rolled by until the fair maiden, Emmeline Cromarty, was of sufficient age to have suitors for her lily-white hand. As we can well believe, after a mere glance in her direction, she was the belle of the whole countryside. Brave gallants from far and near came galloping into the courtyard, and dismounting in feverish haste, cried, 'What ho! is the radiant Emmeline within?' Then the old warden with his clanking keys admitted them, and they stood in rows, that the coquettish damsel might make a selection."

" How ridiculous you are, Sinclair! " said his mother, smiling. " Can't you omit that part? "

" Nay, nay, fair lady. And so, it came to pass, that among the shoals of suitors was one who was far more brave and strong and noble than all the rest. Edgar Hartley——"

Sinclair's voice broke a little as he spoke the name of his revered father. But hiding his emotion, he went on.

" Edgar Hartley wooed and won Emmeline Cromarty, and in the beautiful June of 1880 they were wed and merrily rang the bells. Now while Edgar Hartley was by no means wealthy, he had a fair income, and the fortunes of Cromarty Manor improved. The young couple took up their abode here, and the Dowager Duchess of Cromarty lived with them."

" I'm not a Duchess," interposed Mrs. Cromarty, in her calm way.

" You ought to have been, Grandy," declared Bob. " You look the part, and I'm sure there's a missing title somewhere that belongs to you. Perhaps Uncle Marmaduke concealed it with the rest of his fortune."

"No, dear boy; we are not titled people. But the Cromartys are an old family, and much beloved and respected by all the country round."

"We are so!" declared Bob, with great enthusiasm.

CHAPTER XV

PUZZLING RHYMES

" **A**S I was saying," continued Sinclair, " Mr. and Mrs. Hartley lived happily at Cromarty Manor. Three beautiful children were born to them, who have since grown to be the superior specimens of humanity you see before you. I am the oldest, and, as I may modestly remark, the flower of the family."

" Oh, I don't know," commented Patty, looking affectionately at Mabel.

" Well, anyway, as was only natural, the search for that hidden fortune went on at times. Perhaps a visitor would stir up the interest afresh, and attempts would be made to discover new meaning in Uncle Marmaduke's last words. And it was my father who succeeded in doing this. He sat in the library one day, looking over the old set of Dickens' works, which always had a fascinating air of holding the secret. He had not lived here long then, and was not very familiar with the books on the library shelves, but looking about he discovered another set of Dickens, a much newer set, and the volumes were bound in cloth, but almost entirely covered by a gilded decoration. Wait, I'll show you one."

Sinclair rose, and going into the library, returned in a moment with a copy of " Barnaby Rudge." It was bound in green cloth, but so ornate was the gold tooling that little green could be seen.

" Dickens—gold——" murmured Patty, her eyes shining as she realised the new meaning in the words.

" Yes; and, sure enough that was what Uncle Marmaduke meant. Just think! For fifteen years that set of books had stood untouched on the shelves, while people nearly wore out the older set, hunting for a clue to the fortune! "

" It's great! " declared Patty; " go on! "

" Well, this set of Dickens proved extremely interesting. Between the leaves of the books were papers of all sorts. Bills, deeds, banknotes, memoranda, and even a will."

" Then you had the fortune, at last? "

" No such luck. The banknotes and the few securities in the books amounted to a fair sum, which was gratefully appreciated by my parents, but as to the bulk of the fortune, it only made matters more tantalising than ever."

" Why? " asked Patty.

" One of the papers was a will, properly executed and witnessed, leaving all the fortune of which Uncle Marmaduke died possessed, to my mother. Then, instead of a definite statement of where this money was deposited, were some foolish jingles hinting where to find it. These rhymes would be interesting as an old legend, or in a story book, but to find them instead of a heap of money, was, to say the least, disappointing."

" And did you never find the money? "

" Never. And, of course, now we never will. Remember all this happened twenty years ago. I mean the discovery of the papers. Of course, the money was hidden more than thirty-five years ago."

" And do you mean to say that you people are living here, in your own house, and your own money is hidden here somewhere, and you can't find it? "

" Exactly as you state it."

" Well! *I'd* find it, if I had to tear the whole house down."

" Wait a minute, Miss Impetuosity. We don't think it's in the house."

" Oh, out of doors? "

" You're good at puzzles, I know, but just wait until you hear the directions that came with the package, and I think you'll admit it's a hopeless problem."

" May she see them, Mother? " said Mabel. " Will you get them out for us? "

" Not to-night, dear. I'll show the old papers to Patty, some other time; but now Sinclair can tell her the lines just as well."

" Of all the papers in the books," Sinclair went on, " only two seemed to be directions for finding the money, although others vaguely hinted that the fortune was concealed. And still others gave the impression that Uncle Marmaduke meant to tell mother all about it; but as his death came upon him so suddenly, of course he could not do this. On these two papers are rhymes, which we children have known by heart all our lives. One is:

" ' Great treasure lieth in the poke
    Between the fir trees and the oak.'

" You see uncle was a true poet."

" What does the poke mean? " asked Patty.

Puzzling Rhymes

" Oh, a poke is a pocket; or a hiding-place of any sort. Of course, this information sent father to digging around every fir tree and oak tree on the place. As you know, there are hundreds of both kinds of trees, so the directions can't be called explicit."

" But," said Patty, wrinkling her brow, " it says ' between the fir trees and the oak,' as if it meant a clump of firs and only one big oak."

" Yes; that's what has been surmised. And many a separate oak tree that stands near a group of firs has been thoroughly investigated. But wait; there's another clue. On a separate paper these words are written:

" ' Above the stair, across the hall,
    Between the bedhead and the wall,
  A careful searching will reveal
    The noble fortune I conceal.'

" There, could anything be plainer than that?"

" Then the money is *in* the house!" exclaimed Patty.

" Take your choice. There are the two declarations. It may be he concealed the money in one place, and then transferred it to another.

Or it may be he put part in the ground, and part in the house."

" But, ' between the bedhead and the wall,' is so definite. There are not so very many bed-rooms, you know."

" True enough. And of course, when my father found that paper, he went directly up-stairs, crossed the hall, and so reached Uncle Marmaduke's own bedroom. The furniture had been moved about, but Grandy remembered where the head of the bed stood in Uncle's time. They searched thoroughly, took up floor-ing, took down wainscoting, and all that, to no avail."

" Of course, they tried other ' bedheads '? "

" Yes, tell her about it, Grandy."

" Yes," said Mrs. Cromarty, placidly. " All the bedrooms in the house, even the servants' rooms, were subjected to most careful scrutiny. Although so many years had elapsed, I could remember where the various beds stood when Marmaduke was with us. Behind each, we had the walls sounded, and in some cases, broken into. We even looked for pockets or receptacles of some sort on the backs of the headboards themselves, but never a trace of anything could we find."

Puzzling Rhymes

"It's very exciting!" said Patty; "how can you all be so calm about it? I should think you'd be searching every minute!"

"You must remember, dear," said Mrs. Hartley, "it's an old story to us. At first, we were indeed excited. For several years we searched almost continuously. Then hope began to fail, and our investigations became intermittent. Every now and then we would make a fresh attempt, but invariably repeated failures dampened our enthusiasm."

"It's *so* interesting," sighed Patty. "Can't we get up a little of the old enthusiasm, and do some searching while I'm here?"

"Indeed, we can," cried Bob. "Would you prefer an excavating party, with picks and spades, or an indoor performance in the old bedrooms?"

"Both," declared Patty. "Of course I know how absurd it is to go over the ground that has already been worn threadbare, but—but, oh! if we *could* find it!"

Grandma Cromarty smiled.

"Forgive me, dearie," she said, "but I've heard those sentiments from all my guests to whom we have told the story, for the past thirty-five years; and though I don't want to seem ungrateful for your interest, I feel it my duty to warn you there is no hope."

"Oh, yes there is *hope*, Grandy," said Sinclair, "but there is nothing else. There's no probability, scarcely a possibility, but we'll *never* give up hope."

"Never!" agreed Bob; but Mabel's expression plainly showed that she hadn't the faintest glimmering of a hope.

"It does seem so strange," said Patty, thoughtfully, "to have the two directions, and both so explicit. No, not explicit, they're not that, but both so definite."

"Hardly definite, either," said Bob, "except that they seem to reveal the fact that there *is* a fortune concealed about the place. Oh! it makes me frantic! I feel so helpless."

"There's no use storming about it, Bob, my boy," said his mother. "And, Patty, you mustn't set us down as too mercenary in this matter. But I think you know that we, as a family, long for the means which would enable us to keep up this dear old place as it should be, and not let its beautiful parks and gardens go uncared for and neglected."

"I do know!" cried Patty; "and it makes me furious to think that the money—your own

money—is perhaps within your reach, and yet
—you can't get it! Oh, why didn't Mr. Marmaduke say just where he put it! "

" He did," said Bob, smiling.

" Yes, so he did. Well, I'd tear up every
square foot of ground on the whole estate,
then."

" Remember, Patty," said Sinclair, in his quiet
way, " there are nearly ten thousand acres in
all; and except for meadowlands and water,
there are oaks and firs on nearly every acre.
The fortune itself would scarcely pay for all
that labour."

" Well, then, I'd tear the house to pieces."

" Oh, no you wouldn't," said Mrs. Hartley;
" and beside, that has almost been done. My
husband had so much of the woodwork and
plaster removed, that I almost feared he
would bring the house down about our ears.
And it is such a big, rambling old place,
it is hopeless to think of examining it really
thoroughly."

Patty glanced around at the great hall she was
in. The groined ceiling, with its intricate carvings at the intersections; the cornice carved in
deep relief, with heraldic bosses, and massive
patterns; the tall columns and pilasters; all

seemed part of an old monument which it would be desecration to break into.

"I wonder where it is," she said; "indoors or out."

"I think it's out of doors," said Sinclair. "I think uncle hid it in the house first, and then wrote his exquisite poem about the poke. Perhaps it was merely a pocket of leather or canvas, that hung behind the headboard of his own bed. In that case all prying into the walls would mean nothing. Then, I think, as that was only a temporary hiding-place, he later buried it in the ground between some special oak tree and fir tree, or trees. I think, too, he left, or meant to leave some more of his poetry to tell which trees, but owing to his sudden taking off, he didn't do this."

"Sinclair," said Bob, "as our American friend, Mr. Dooley, says, 'Yer opinions is inthrestin', but not convincin'.' As opinions, they're fine; but I wish I had some facts. If uncle had only left a cryptogram or a cipher, I'd like it better than all that rhymed foolishness."

"Perhaps it isn't foolishness," said Patty; "I think, with Sinclair, it's likely Mr. Marmaduke wrote the indoor one first, and then changed the hiding-place and wrote the other. But how could he do all this hiding and rehiding without being seen?"

"I went up to London every season," said Mrs. Cromarty; "and, of course, took Emmeline with me. Marmaduke always stayed here, and thus had ample opportunity to do what he would. Indeed, he usually had great goings-on while we were away. One year, he had the Italian garden laid out. Another year, he had a new porter's lodge built. This was done the last year of his life, and as he had masons around so much at that time, repairing the cellars and all that, we thought later, that he might have had a hiding-place arranged in the wall behind the head of his bed. But, if so, we never could find it."

"And have you dug under the trees much?" persisted Patty, who could not accept the hopelessness of the others.

"Dug!" exclaimed Bob, "I've blistered my hands by the hour. I've viewed fir trees and oaks, until I know every one on the place by heart. I've trudged a line from oaks to firs, and starting in the middle, I've dug both ways. But I'm nearly ready to give up. Not quite, though. I'm making a thorough search of all the books in the library, on the chance of find-

ing some other message. But there are such a
lot of books! I've been at it for three years
now, off and on, and I'm only three-quarters
way round. And not a paper yet, except a few
old letters and bills."

"I'll help you, Bob," said Patty; " oh, I'd love
to do something toward the search, even if I
don't find a thing. I'll begin to-morrow. You
tell me what books you've done."

" I will, indeed. I'll be jolly glad to have
help. And you can do as much as you
like, before your young enthusiasm wears
off."

" I'll do it, gladly," said Patty, and then they
discovered that the evening had flown away,
and it was bedtime.

As they went upstairs, Mabel followed Patty
to her room and sat down for a little good-night
chat.

Patty's eyes were shining with excitement, and
as she took off her hair ribbon, and folded it
round her hand, she said:

" Even if we don't find anything, you'll be no
worse off, and it's such fun to hunt."

" They didn't tell you all, Patty," said Mabel,
in a pathetic tone, and Patty turned quickly to
her friend.

Puzzling Rhymes

"Why, what do you mean?"

"I mean this. Of course, we've never been rich, and we've never been able to do for the place what ought to be done for it; but we have been able to live here. And now—now, if we can't get any more money, we—we can't stay here! Oh, Patty!"

Patty's arms went round Mabel, as the poor child burst into tears.

"Yes," she said, sobbing, "some of mother's business interests have failed—it's all come on lately, I don't entirely understand it—but, anyway, we may soon have to leave Cromarty, and oh, Patty, how *could* we live anywhere else? and what's worse, how *could* we have any one else living here?"

"Leave Cromarty Manor! Where you've all lived so long—I mean your ancestors and all! Why, Mabel, you can't do that!"

"But we'll have to. We haven't money enough to pay the servants—or, at least, we won't have, soon."

"Are you sure of all this, dear? Does Mrs. Cromarty expect to go away?"

"It's all uncertain. We don't know. But mother's lawyer thinks we'd better sell or let the place. Of course we won't sell it, but it would be almost as bad to let it. Think of strangers here! "

" I can't think of such a thing! It seems impossible. But perhaps matters may turn out better than you think. Perhaps you won't have to go."

" That's what Sinclair says—and mother. But I'm sure the worst will happen."

" Now, Mabel, stop that! I won't let you look on the dark side. And, anyway, you're not to think any more about it to-night. You won't sleep a wink if you get nervous and worried. Now put it out of your mind, and let's talk about the croquet party to-morrow at Grace Meredith's. How are we going over? "

" You and I are to drive in the pony cart, and the others will go in the carriage."

" That will be lovely. Now, what shall we wear? "

Thus, tactfully, Patty led Mabel's thoughts away from her troubles, for the time, at least, and when the two friends parted for the night, they both went healthily and happily to sleep.

CHAPTER XVI

THE CROQUET PARTY

THE next afternoon the two girls started in the pony cart for the Merediths.

Patty loved to play croquet, and though it greatly amused her to hear the English people pronounce the word as if it were spelled *croky*, yet not to appear peculiar, she spoke it that way too.

The party was a large one, and the games were arranged somewhat after the fashion of a tournament.

Patty's partner was Tom Meredith, and as he played a fairly good game they easily beat their first opponents.

But later on they found themselves matched against Mabel Hartley and a young man named Jack Stanton. Mr. Stanton was an expert, and Mabel played the best game Patty had ever seen a girl play.

" It's no use," said Patty, good-naturedly, as they began the game, " Tom and I never can win against you two."

"Don't despair," said Tom, encouragingly, "There's many a slip, you know."

The game progressed until, when Tom and Patty were about three-quarters of the way around, Mabel was passing through her last wicket and Mr. Stanton was a "rover."

"Be careful, now," said Mr. Stanton, as Mabel aimed to send her ball through the arch. "It's a straight shot, and a long shot, and you're liable to touch the post."

And that's just what happened. As Mabel's swift, clear stroke sent the ball straight through the wicket, it went spinning on and hit squarely the home stake.

"Jupiter! that's bad luck!" exclaimed Jack Stanton. "They'll jolly well beat us now. But never mind, perhaps I can slip through yet."

But he couldn't. The fact that they had two plays to his one, gave Patty and Tom a great advantage.

Tom was a clever manager, and Patty followed his directions implicitly. So they played a defensive game, and spent much time keeping Stanton's ball away from the positions he desired. The result was that Tom and Patty won, but their success was really owing to Mabel's mistake in going out.

The Croquet Party

The test was to win two games out of three, so with one game in favor of Patty's side they began the next.

Patty was considered a good croquet player in America, but in England the rules of the game, as well as the implements, were so different that it seriously impeded her progress.

The wickets were so narrow that the ball could barely squeeze through if aimed straight, and a side shot through one was impossible.

But all this added to the zest, and it was four very eager young people who strove for the victory.

The second game went easily to Mabel and Jack Stanton, and then the third, the decisive one, was begun. According to the laws of the tournament, this was the final game. The opponents had already vanquished all the other contestants, and now, pitted against each other, were playing for the prize.

Patty knew in her heart she would be glad to have Mabel win it, and yet, so strong was her love of games, and so enthusiastic her natural desire to succeed, that she tried her best to beat the third game.

All played conservatively. The partners kept together, and progressed evenly. Toward the

last Jack and Mabel began to creep ahead.
Tom saw this, and said to Patty: " This is our
last chance; if we plod on like this, they'll calmly
walk out and leave us. Unless we can make a
brilliant dash of some sort, we are beaten."

" I don't believe I can," said Patty, looking
doubtfully at her ball. " It's my turn, and unless I can hit Mabel's ball, clear across the
grounds, I can't do anything."

" That's just it. You *must* hit Mabel's ball."
So Patty aimed carefully, and sent her ball
spinning over the ground toward Mabel's, and
missed it by a hair's breadth!

" Goody! " cried Mabel, and hitting Patty's
ball, she roqueted it back where it had come
from.

" Now here's our very lastest chance," said
Tom, with a groan of despair. " And I'm sure,
Patty, I won't do any better than you did."

Nor did he. Although not far from Jack's
ball, at which he aimed, there was a wicket in
the way, which sent his own ball glancing off at
an angle, and he did not hit his opponent.

A minute more, and Jack skilfully sent Mabel's
ball and then his own against the home stake,
and the game was over.

The onlookers crowded up and congratulated

the winners, and offered condolence to Patty and Tom. Patty smiled, and responded merrily. She did not try to lay the blame on the unusual shaped wickets, or short, heavy mallets. She declared that the best players had won, and that she was satisfied. And indeed she was.

When she saw the lovely prize that was given to Mabel, she was deeply thankful that she hadn't won it. It was a white parasol, of silk and chiffon, with a pearl handle. A really exquisite, dainty affair, and just the very thing Mabel had wanted, but couldn't afford to buy. As for Patty herself, she had several parasols, and so was delighted that Mabel had won.

But though she truly preferred that Mabel should have the prize, she felt a little chagrined at losing the contest, for like all people who are fond of games and sports, Patty loved to win.

These feelings, though, she successfully concealed, and gave Mabel very sincere and loving congratulations. Mr. Stanton's prize was a pretty scarf pin, and Tom Meredith loudly bewailed his own misfortune in losing this. Though, really, as the tournament was at his own home, he would not have taken the prize had he won it, but would have passed it on to the one with the next highest record.

The victors were cheered and applauded, and were then led in triumph to the pretty tent where tea was being served.

It Patty had had a shadow of regret that she had not been the honoured one, it was lost sight of in her gladness that it fell to Mabel's lot.

"You're a plucky one," said Tom Meredith, who was observing her closely. "You're a good loser, aren't you?"

"I don't know," said Patty, thoughtfully. "I want to be, but do you know, I just love to win contests or games. And when I lose— I'm ashamed to say it—but I do feel put out."

"Of course you do! That's only natural. And that's why I say you're a good loser. If you didn't care tuppence whether you won or not, it wouldn't be much to your credit to look smiling and pleasant when you lose. But since you *do* care, a whole lot, you're a jolly plucky girl to take it so well. Now, what can I get for you? An ice?"

"Yes, please," said Patty, really gratified at Tom's appreciative words.

"How long are you staying with the Hartleys?" Tom asked, as, returning with ices, he found cosy seats at a small table for himself and Patty.

The Croquet Party

" Two or three weeks longer, I think. But I shall hate to go away, for I've become so interested in their ' mystery,' that I can't stop trying to solve it."

" Oh, you mean that old affair of the hidden fortune. I don't believe there's any at all. I think the old man who pretended to hide it was merely guying them."

" Oh, no! That can't be. Why, it all sounds so real and natural. The story of the hiding, I mean."

" Yes, but why should he want to hide it? Why not bank it decently, like other people? "

" Oh, because he was eccentric. People who are naturally queer or freakish are always hiding things. And I know it's silly of me, but I'm going to try to find that money."

" I've lots of faith in your energy and perseverance, but I can't think you'll succeed in that job. Better try something easier."

" I don't think I can say I expect to succeed. But I'm going to try—and—who can tell what might happen? "

" Who, indeed? But you know, of course, that the Cromarty people have been hunting it for nearly forty years."

" Yes," said Patty, and her eyes fairly blazed

with determination, "yes—but I am an American!"

Tom Meredith shouted with laughter.

"Good for you, little Stars and Stripes!" he cried. "I've always heard of the cleverness of the Yankees, but if you can trace the Cromarty fortune, I'll believe you a witch, for sure. Aren't there witches in that New England of yours?"

"I believe there used to be. And my ancestors, some of them, were Salem people. That may be where I get my taste for divination and solving problems. I just love puzzles of all sorts, and if the old Cromarty gentleman had only left a cipher message, it would have been fun to puzzle it out."

"He did leave messages of some sort, didn't he? Maybe they are more subtle than you think."

"I've been wondering about that. They might mean something entirely different from what they sound like; but I can't see any light that way. 'The headboard of a bed against a wall,' is pretty practical, and doesn't seem to mean anything else. And the oak trees and fir trees are there in abundance. But that's the trouble with them, there are so many."

The Croquet Party

" Go on, and do all you can, my child. You'll get over it the sooner, if you work hard on it at first. We've all been through it. Nearly everybody in this part of the country has tried at one time or another to guess the Cromarty riddle."

" But I'm the first American to try," insisted Patty, with a twinkle in her eye.

" Quite so, Miss Yankee Doodle Doo; and I wish you success where my own countrymen have failed."

Tom said this with such a nice, kindly air that Patty felt a little ashamed of her own vaunting attitude. But sometimes Patty showed a decided tendency to over-assuredness in her own powers, and though she tried to correct it, it would spring up now and again. Then the Hartley boys joined them, and all discussion of the missing fortune was dropped.

It was soon time to take leave, and as it was already twilight, Sinclair proposed that he should drive Patty home in the pony cart, and Mabel should return in the carriage.

Mabel quite agreed to this, saying that after her croquet, she did not care to drive. The road lay through a lovely bit of country, and Patty enjoyed the drive home with Sinclair.

Patty's Friends

She always liked to talk with him, he was so gentle and kindly. While not so merry as Bob or as Tom Meredith, Sinclair was an interesting talker, and Patty always felt that she was benefited by his conversation.

He told her much about the country as they drove along, described the life and work of the villagers, and pointed out buildings or other objects of interest.

They passed several fine estates, whose towering mansions could be seen half hidden by trees, or boldly placed on a summit.

"But no place is as beautiful as Cromarty," said Sinclair, and Patty entirely agreed with them.

"Is it true that you may have to leave it?" she asked, thinking it wiser to refer to it casually.

Sinclair frowned.

"Who's been talking to you?" he said; "Mabel, I suppose. Well, yes, there is a chance that we'll have to let it for a term of years. I hope not, but I can't tell yet. But even if so, it will be only temporary. As soon as I get fairly established in my career, I hope to make money enough to take care of it all. A few years hence, when I'm on my feet, and Bob's through college, it will be easier all round. But if some business troubles that are now impending don't blow over, there'll be no income to keep things going, and we'll have to—to——— But that *shan't* happen! "

Sinclair spoke almost desperately, and Patty saw his fingers clench around the reins he was holding.

" I wonder," said Patty slowly, for she was not quite sure how what she was about to say would be received. " I wonder, Sinclair, if we're not good friends enough, you and I, for me to speak plainly to you."

The young man gave her a quick, earnest glance.

" Go on," he said, briefly.

" It's only this," said Patty, still hesitating, " my father has lots of money—couldn't you— couldn't he lend you some? "

Sinclair looked at her squarely now, and spoke in low, stern tones.

" Never suggest such a thing again. The Cromartys do not borrow."

" Not even from a friend? " said Patty, softly.

" Not even from a friend," repeated Sinclair, but his voice was more gentle. " You don't understand, I suppose," he went on, " but we would

leave Cromarty for ever before we would stay
on such terms."

"No," said Patty, "I don't understand. I
should think you'd be as glad to accept a friend's
help as he would be to offer it."

"If you'd do me a real kindness, Patty, you'll
never even mention such an idea again. I know
you mean well and I thank you, but it's absolutely impossible."

"Then there's only one other way out of the
difficulty," said Patty, with an effort at light-
ness; "and that's to find your buried fortune."

"Ah, that would be a help," cried Sinclair,
also assuming a gayer tone. "If you'll help us
to do that, I'll set up a memorial tablet to your
cleverness."

"Where will you set it? Between the fir trees
and the oak?"

"Yes, if you find the fortune there."

"But if I find it behind the headboard, that's
no sort of a place for a tablet!"

"You can choose your own spot for your Roll
of Fame, and I'll see to it that the memorial is a
worthy one."

"And will you put fresh flowers on it every
day?"

"Yes, indeed; for if—I mean *when*, you find

the fortune for us, the gardens will have immediate attention."

"Then I must set to work at once," said Patty, with pretended gravity, but in her heart she registered a mental vow to try in earnest to fulfil the promise given in jest.

CHAPTER XVII

THE GRIFFIN AND THE ROSE

ALTHOUGH the Hartleys had practically given up all hope of ever finding the hidden money, they couldn't help being imbued with Patty's enthusiasm.

Indeed, it took little to rouse the sleeping fires of interest that never were entirely extinguished.

But though they talked it over by the hour there seemed to be nothing to do but talk.

One day, Patty went out all by herself, determined to see if she couldn't find some combination of an oak tree and a group of firs that would somehow seem especially prominent.

But after looking at a score or more of such combinations, she realised that task was futile.

She looked at the ground under some of them, but who could expect a mark of any kind on the ground after nearly forty years? No. Unless Mr. Marmaduke Cromarty had marked his hiding-place with a stone or iron plate, it would probably never be found by his heirs. Search in the house was equally unsatisfactory. What availed it to scan a wall or a bedstead that had been scrutinised for years by eager, anxious eyes? And then Patty set her wits to work. She tried to think where an erratic old gentleman would secrete his wealth. And she was forced to admit that the most natural place was in the ground on his estate, the location to be designated by some obscure message. And surely, the message was obscure enough!

She kept her promise to help Bob in his self-appointed task of going through all the books in the library. This was no small piece of work, for it was not enough to shake each book, and let loose papers, if any, drop out. Some of the old papers had been found pinned to leaves, and so each book must be run through in such a way that every page could be glanced at.

Nor was this a particularly pleasant task. For Mrs. Hartley had made it a rule that when her own children went over the old books, they were to dust them as they went along. Thus, she said, at least some good would be accomplished, though no hidden documents might be found.

Of course, she did not request Patty to do this, but learning of the custom, Patty insisted on doing it, and many an hour she spent in the old library, clad in apron and dust-cap. Her progress was rather slow, for book-loving Patty often became absorbed in the old volumes, and dropping down on the window-seat, or the old steps to the gallery, would read away, oblivious to all else till some one came to hunt for her.

At last, one day, her patient search met a reward. In an old book she found several of what were beyond all doubt Mr. Marmaduke Comarty's papers.

Without looking at them closely, Patty took the book straight to Mrs. Cromarty.

"Dear me!" said the old lady, putting on her glasses. "Have we really found something? I declare I'm quite nervous over it. Emmeline, you read them."

Mrs. Hartley was a bit excited, too, and as for Patty and Mabel, they nearly went frantic at their elders' slowness in opening the old and yellow papers.

There were several letters, a few bills, and some hastily-scribbled memoranda. The letters and bills were of no special interest, but on one of the small bits of paper was another rhymed couplet that seemed to indicate a direction.

It read:

The Griffin and the Rose

"Where the angry griffin shows,
Ruthless, tear away the rose."

"Oh," exclaimed Patty, "it's another direction how to get the fortune! Oh, Mabel, it will be all right yet! Oh, where is the angry griffin? Is it over a rosebush? You're only to pull up the rosebush, and there you are!"

Mabel looked bewildered. So did the older ladies.

"Speak, somebody!" cried Patty, dancing about in excitement. "Isn't there any angry griffin? There must be!"

"That's the trouble," said Mrs. Hartley; "there are so many of them. Why, there are angry griffins on the gates, over the lodge doors, on the marbles in the gardens, and all over the house."

"Of course there are," said Mabel. "You must have noticed them, Patty. There's one now," and she pointed to a bit of wood carving over the door frame of the room they were in.

"I don't care! It means something, I know it does," declared Patty. "We'll work it out yet. I wish the boys were home."

"They'll soon be here," said Mrs. Cromarty.

"I can't help thinking that it does mean something—Marmaduke was very fond of roses, and it would be just like him to plant a rosebush over his buried treasure."

"That's it," cried Patty. "Now, where is there a rosebush growing, and one of the angry griffins near it?"

"There probably are some in the rose garden," said Mrs. Cromarty. "I don't remember any, though."

"Come on, Mabel," said Patty, "let's go and look. I can't wait another minute!"

Away flew the two girls, and for the next hour they hovered about the rosebushes with more energy than is often shown by the busiest of bees.

"I wish old Uncle Marmaduke had been less of a poet," said Mabel, as they sat down a moment to rest, "and more of a—a——"

"More straightforward," suggested Patty. "If he'd only written a few words of plain prose, and left it with his lawyer, all this trouble needn't have been."

"Well, I suppose he did intend to make it plain before he died, but he went off so suddenly. Oh, here are the boys."

Sinclair and Bob came bounding down toward

the rose garden, followed more sedately by their mother and grandmother.

"Not a sign of a griffin a-sniffin' of a rose," said Patty, disconsolately.

"Oh, you haven't looked all round yet," said Bob. "It's such fun to have something to look for besides fir trees and beds, I'm going to make a close search."

"Of course," said Sinclair, "the same rose bush wouldn't be here now that was here thirty or forty years ago."

"But it would have been renewed," said Mrs. Cromarty. "We've always tried to keep the flowers as nearly as possible the same."

"Then here goes to interview every griffin on the place," declared Bob. "Jolly of old uncle to mark the spot with a rosebush and a griffin. That's what I call decent of him. And you're a wonder, Patty, to find the old paper."

"Oh, that's nothing," said Patty. "I just followed your orders about the books. If you'd kept at it yourself, you'd have found the same book."

"I s'pose so. But I'm glad you helped the good work along. Oh, dear! no rosebush seems to be near a griffin; and the griffins seem positively afraid of the rosebushes."

And try as they would, no angry griffin could they find, with a rosebush near it. Griffins there were in plenty; both angry and grinning. Also were there plenty of roses, but they were arranged in well-laid-out beds, and in no case were guarded or menaced by angry griffins.

"Never mind," said Sinclair, as they returned to the house for dinner, " it's something to work on. I shall stay at home to-morrow and try to find that particular rosebush, or the place where it used to be."

" Maybe it's a stone rose," said Patty, as she touched a rose carved in stone that was part of an ornamental urn whose handles were the heads of angry griffins. Sinclair stared at her.

"You're right," he said, slowly, as if grasping a great thought. " It's much more likely to be a rose of stone or marble, and when that's ruthlessly torn away the secret will be revealed. Oh, mother, there *is* hope! "

Patty had never seen the placid Sinclair so excited, and they all went to their rooms to get ready for dinner, with a feeling that something was going to happen. Conversation at dinner was all on the engrossing subject.

Everybody made suggestions, and everybody recalled various partly-forgotten griffins in odd nooks and corners, each being sure that was " just the place uncle would choose!"

After dinner, the young people were anxious to go out and search more, but it had begun to rain, so they all went into the library and again scrutinised the old papers Patty had found.

They looked through more books, too, but found nothing further of interest.

At last, wearied with the hunt, Patty threw herself into a big armchair and declared she would do no more that night.

" I should say not," said Bob. " You've done quite enough in giving us this new start."

Although, as Patty had said, the looking through all the old books was Bob's plan, he generously gave her the credit of this new find. Sinclair threw himself on a long leather couch, and began to sing softly some of their nonsense songs, as he often did when tired out. The others joined, and for a time the fortune was left to take care of itself.

Very pleasant were the four fresh young voices, and the elders listened gladly to their music.

In the middle of a song, Patty stopped, and sat bolt upright, her eyes staring at a door opposite her as if she had never seen it before.

Patty's Friends

"Gracious, goodness! Patty," said Mabel, "what is the matter?"

"What is it, little one?" said Sinclair, still humming the refrain of the interrupted song.

Patty pointed to the door, or rather to the elaborately carved door frame, and said slowly, "I've been reading a lot in the old architecture books—and they often used to have secret hiding places in the walls. And look at that door frame! There's an angry griffin on one jamb, and a smiling griffin on the other, and under each is a rose. That is it's a five-leafed blossom, a sort of conventional flower that they always call a rose in architecture."

"Though I suppose," said Sinclair, "by any other name it would look as sweet. Patty, my child, you're dreaming. That old carving is as solid as Gibraltar and that old griffin isn't very angry anyway. He just looks rather purse proud and haughty."

"But it's the only griffin that's near a rose," persisted Patty. "And he is angry, compared to the happy-looking griffin opposite to him."

"I believe the girl is right," said Bob, who was already examining the carvings in question. "The rose doesn't look movable, exactly, but it is not quite like this other rose. It's more deeply cut."

By this time all had clustered about the door frame, and one after another poked and pushed at the wooden rose.

"There's something in it," persisted Bob. "In the idea, I mean. If there's a secret hiding-place in that upright carved beam, that rose is the key to it. See how deeply it's cut in, compared to the other; and I can almost see a crack all round it, as if it could be removed. May I try to get it out, Grandy?"

"Certainly, my boy. We mustn't leave a stone unturned."

"A rose unturned, you mean. Clair, what shall we ruthlessly tear it away with? I hate to take a chisel to this beautiful old door."

"Try a corkscrew," said Mabel.

"You mean a gimlet," said Bob. "That's a good idea."

Fetching a gimlet, he bored a hole right in the centre of the carved blossom, but though it turned and creaked a little it wouldn't come out.

"It must come," said Sinclair. "It turns, so that proves it's meant to be movable. It probably has some hinge or spring that is rusted, and so it doesn't work as it ought to. We'll have to take hammer and chisel; shall we, Grandy?"

The boys were deferential to Mrs. Cromarty, for they well knew that she was tired of having the old house torn up to no avail. But surely this was an important development.

"Yes, indeed, boys. If your uncle's words mean anything, they mean that it must be ruthlessly torn away, if removed at all."

For quite ten minutes the two boys worked away with their tools, endeavouring to mar the carving as little as might be, but resolved to succeed in their undertaking. At last the wooden rose fell out in their hands, leaving a round opening.

Peering in, Sinclair saw a small iron knob, which seemed to be part of a rusty spring.

Greatly excited, he tried to push or turn it, but couldn't move it.

"Anyway, we're getting warm," he cried, and his glowing face corroborated his words.

The boys took turns in working at the stubborn spring, trying with forceps and pincers to move it, until at last something seemed to give way, and the whole front of the door jamb fell out as one panel.

Behind it was a series of small pigeon holes

⦁ne above the other, all filled with neatly piled papers.

Though yellow with age, the papers were care-'fully folded, labelled, and dated.

" Patty ! " cried Mabel, as she embraced her friend, " you've found our fortune for us ! "

" Don't be too sure," said Patty, laughing, and almost crying at the same time, so excited was she. " Your Uncle Marmaduke was of such uncertain ways I shouldn't wonder if these were merely more files of his immortal verse."

" They're bills," declared Sinclair, as he ran over a packet he took from a shelf.

" Let's look them all over systematically," said Bob. " Let's all sit round the table, and one of us read out what the paper is about. Then if we come to anything important, we'll all know it at once."

This plan was adopted, and Sinclair, as the oldest, was chosen to read. He sat at the head of the long library table, and the others were at either side.

But the packets of bills, though interesting in a general way, had no bearing on the great question of the fortune. The papers were all bills.

" Not even a bit of poetry," sighed Patty, as

Sinclair laid aside one after another of the receipted bills for merchandise, household goods, clothing, and labour.

"These might interest a historian," said Sinclair, " as they throw some light on the prices of goods at that time. But we'll keep on, we may come to something of interest yet."

"I hope so," said Bob. "I'm so anxious, that nothing less than a straight direction to the fortune would satisfy me."

"Well, here's something," said Sinclair, "whatever it may mean."

The paper he had just unfolded was a mason's bill, containing only one item. The bill was made out in due form, by one Martin Campbell, and was properly receipted as paid. And its single item read:

"To constructing one secret pocket . . . . . Three Guineas."

"Oh!" cried Patty, breathless with excitement. "Then there *is* a secret pocket, or poke as your exasperating uncle calls it."

"There must be," said Sinclair; "and now that we know that, we're going to find it. Of course, we assumed there was one, but we had only that foolish doggerel to prove it. Now this regular bill establishes it as a fact beyond all doubt. Do you know this Martin Campbell, Grandy?"

"I know there was a mason by that name, who worked here several times for your uncle. He came down from Leicester, but of course I know nothing more of him."

"We'll find him!" declared Bob. "We'll make him give up the secret of the pocket."

"Maybe he's dead by this time," said Sinclair. "Was he an old man, Grandy?"

"I don't know, my dear. I never saw him. He worked here when I was away in London. I fear, however, he is not alive now."

"Oh, perhaps he is. It was only about thirty-five years ago, or forty, that he built this 'secret pocket.' Thirty-eight, to be exact. The date on the bill proves that."

"Well, to-morrow you must go to see him," said Mrs. Hartley, rising. "But now, my children, you must go to bed. You can't learn any more to-night, and to-morrow we will pick up the broken thread. Patty, my dear child, you are doing a great deal for us."

"It isn't anything yet," said Patty, "but oh, if it only leads to something, I shall be so glad!"

CHAPTER XVIII

THE OLD CHIMNEY-PIECE

BUT Sinclair's search for the old mason in Leicester was absolutely unsuccessful. He learned that Martin Campbell had died many years ago, and had left no direct descendants. A cousin of the old mason told Sinclair all this, and said, too, that there were no books or papers or accounts of the dead man left in existence.

So Sinclair returned home, disappointed but not entirely discouraged.

"We'll find it yet," he said to Patty. "We have proof of a hiding-place, now we must discover it."

"We will!" declared Patty. "But it's so exasperating not to know whether the old mason built that 'pocket' indoors or out."

"Out, I think," said Sinclair. "It's probably a sunken bin or vault of brick, made water-tight, and carefully concealed."

"Yes, it's certainly carefully concealed," Patty agreed.

The Old Chimney-piece

Sinclair was entitled to a fortnight's vacation from his law studies, and he arranged to take it at this time. For now that the interest was revived, all were eager to make search all the time.

" Let's be systematic about it," said Bob, " and divide the estate up into sections. Then let's examine each section in turn."

This sounded well, but it was weary work. In the wooded land, especially, it was hopeless to look for any indicatory mark beneath the undergrowth of forty years. But each morning the four young people started out with renewed determination to keep at it, at any rate.

On rainy days they searched about the house. Having found one secret panel, they hoped for more, and the boys went about tapping the walls or carved woodwork here and there, listening for a hollow sound.

Bob and Patty went on searching the books. But though a number of old papers were found they were of no value. Incidentally, Patty was acquiring a store of information of various sorts. Though too eager in her work to sit down and read any book through, she scanned many pages here and there, and learned much that was interesting and useful. Especially did she like books that described the old castles and abbeys of England. There were many of these books, both architectural and historical, and Patty lingered over the illustrations, and let her eyes run hastily over the pages of description.

One afternoon she sat cross-legged, in Turk fashion, on the library floor, absorbed in an account of the beautiful old mansion known as " Audley End." The description so interested her that she read on and on, and in her perusal she came to this sentence:

" There are other curious relics, among them the chair of Alexander Pope, and the carved oak head of Cromwell's bed, converted into a chimney-piece."

Anything in reference to the headboard of a bedstead caught Patty's attention, and she read the paragraph over again.

" Sinclair," she called, but he had gone elsewhere, and did not hear her.

Patty looked around at the mantel or chimney-piece in the library, but it was so evidently a part of the plan of wall decoration, that it could not possibly have been anything else.

Patty sighed. " It would have been so lovely," she thought to herself, " if it only had been a bedhead, made into a mantel, for then that

The Old Chimney-piece

bothering old man could easily have tucked his
money between it and the wall."

And then, though Patty's thoughts came slowly,
they came surely, and she remembered that in
the great hall, or living-room, the mantel was a
massive affair of carved oak.

Half bewildered, Patty dropped the book,
jumped up, and went to the door of the hall.
No one was there, and the girl was glad of it,
for if she really was on the eve of a great discovery she wanted to be alone at first.

As she entered the room, the lines came to her
mind:

" Above the stair, across the hall,
Between the bedhead and the wall,"

and she noticed that the chimney-piece stood on
a sort of wide platform, which extended across
that whole end of the hall. Could it be that
Mr. Marmaduke had meant above this platform, calling it a stair, which ran across the
great hall? For years they had taken the direction to mean " up the staircase," and " across
the corridor," or hall which led to the bed-
rooms.

Slowly, almost as if afraid, Patty crossed the

hall, stepped up on the platform, and examined the old chimney-piece. She couldn't tell, positively, but surely, surely it looked as if it *might* once have been the headboard of an ancient bed. It certainly was different in its workmanship from the wood carving that decorated the apartment.

The top of it was well above her head, but might it not be that the old rhyme meant between *this* bedhead and the wall?

Here they had never looked. It must be that it was not generally known that this mantel was, or had been, a bedhead.

Still, as if in a daze, Patty went and sat in a chair facing the old chimney-piece, and wondered. She intended to call the others in a moment, but first she wanted to enjoy alone the marvel of her own discovery.

As she sat there, scrutinising every detail of the room, the lines kept repeating themselves in her brain:

" Above the stair, across the hall,
    Between the bedhead and the wall."

If the secret pocket was between that bedhead and the wall, it was certainly above the stair

across the hall! Why had that stair or platform been built across the hall? It was a peculiar arrangement.

This question Patty gave up, but she thought
it might well have been done when the bedhead
was set up there, in order to make the chimney-
piece higher and so more effective.

Patty had learned something of architecture in
her library browsings.

Above the high mantel was a large painting.
It was a landscape and showed a beautiful bit
of scenery without buildings or people. In the
foreground were several distinct trees of noble
proportions.

" They're firs," said Patty to herself, for she
had become thoroughly familiar with fir trees.

And then, like a flash, through her brain came
the words:

" Great treasure lieth in the poke
Between the fir trees and the oak."

The secret was revealed! Patty knew it!

Beside the bedhead evidence, it was clear to
her mind that " Between the fir trees and the
oak," meant between these painted fir trees and
the old carved oak mantel. Grasping the arms

of her chair, she sat still a minute trying to take it all in, and then looked about for something to stand on that she might examine the top of the old mantel-shelf.

But her next quick thought was, that that was not her right. Those to whom the fortune belonged must make the investigation themselves.

"Sinclair," called Patty, again; "Mabel, Mrs. Hartley, where are you all?"

Bob responded first, and seeing by Patty's excited face that she had discovered something important, he went in search of the others.

At last they were all gathered in the great hall, and Patty's sense of the dramatic proved too strong to allow her to make her announcement simply.

"People," she said, "I have made a discovery. That is, I think I have. If I am right, the Cromarty fortune is within your grasp. If I am wrong—well, in that case, we'll begin all over again."

"Tell us about your new find," said Sinclair, selecting a comfortable chair, and sitting down as if for a long session. "Is it another mason's bill?"

Nobody minded being chaffed about searching

or finding, for the subject was treated jocosely as well as seriously.

Patty stood on the platform in front of the carved oak chimney-piece, and addressed her audience, who listened, half laughing, half eager.

" What is this on which I stand? " she demanded.

" A rug," replied Mabel, promptly.

" I mean beneath the rug? "

" The floor."

" No, it isn't! What is this—this construction across the room? "

" A platform," put in Bob, willing to help her along.

" Yes. But what else could it be called? I'm in earnest."

" A step," suggested Sinclair.

" Yes, a step; but couldn't it be called a stair? "

" It *could* be," said Bob, " but I don't believe it is one."

" But suppose your erratic uncle chose to call it that."

" Oh," laughed Bob, " you mean the stair in the poem."

" I do. I mean the stair across the hall."

"What! Oh, I say, Patty, now you're jumbling up the sense."

"No, I'm not. I'm straightening out the sense. Suppose Mr. Marmaduke meant ' above the stair across the hall,' and meant this stair and this hall."

"Yes, but go on," said Sinclair; "next comes the bedhead."

"That's my discovery!" announced Patty, with what was truly forgivable triumph.

"This carved oak chimney-piece is, I have reason to believe, the headboard of some magnificent, ancient bed."

"Patty Fairfield!" cried Sinclair, jumping up, and reaching her side with two bounds. "You've struck it! What a girl you are!"

"Wait a minute," said Patty, pushing him back; "I'm entitled to a hearing. Take your seat again, sir, until I unfold the rest of the tale."

Patty was fairly quivering with excitement. Her cheeks glowed, and her eyes shone, and her voice trembled as she went on.

Mabel, with clasped hands, just sat and looked at her. The elder ladies were plainly bewildered, and Bob was trying hard to sit still.

"I read in an old book," Patty went on, "how

somebody else used a carved headboard for a chimney-piece, and I wondered if this mightn't be one. And it surely looks like it. And then I wondered if ' above the stair across the hall ' mightn't mean this platform across this hall. And I think it does. But that's not all. My really important discovery is this."

Patty's voice had sunk to a thrilling whisper, and she addressed herself to Mrs. Cromarty, as she continued.

" I think the other rhyme, the one that says the fortune is concealed ' between the fir trees and the oak,' refers to this same place, and means between the painting of fir trees, which hangs over the mantel, and—the oak mantel itself ! "

With a smiling bow, Patty stepped down from the platform, and taking a seat by old Mrs. Cromarty, nestled in that lady's loving arms. The two boys made a spring for the mantel, but paused simultaneously to grasp both Patty's hands in theirs and nearly shake her arms off. Then they left the heroine of the hour to Mabel and Mrs. Hartley and began to investigate the chimney piece.

" ' Between the fir trees and the oak ' ! " exclaimed Bob. " Great, isn't it ! And here for thirty-five years we Cromarty dubs have thought that meant real trees! To think it took a Yankee to tell us! Oh, Patty, Patty, we'll take down that historic painting and put up a tablet to the honour of Saint Patricia. For you surely deserve canonisation!"

"'Between the bedhead and the wall,'" ruminated Sinclair. "Well, here goes for finding an opening."

Clambering up on stools, both boys examined the place where the mantel shelf touched the wall. The ornate carvings of the mantel left many interstices where coins or notes might be dropped through, yet they were by no means conspicuous enough to attract the attention of any one not looking for them.

"Crickets!" cried Bob. "There's a jolly place for the precious poke to be located. I'm going down cellar to see if I can find traces of that mason's work. Come on, Clair."

The two boys flew off, and the ladies remained discussing the wonderful discovery, and examining the old chimney-piece.

"I can see it was a bedhead now," said Mabel; "but I never suspected it before. What a splendid mantel it makes. Didn't you ever hear its history, Grandy?"

The Old Chimney-piece

"No, dear. It must have been put there when the house was built, I think. Though, of course, it may have been added later. But it was all before my time. I married your grandfather Cromarty and came here to live in 1855. The building and decorations then were all just as they are now, except for such additions as Marmaduke made. He may have had that mantel set up in earlier years—I don't know. He was very fond of antique carvings."

Back came the boys from the cellar.

"The whole chimney is bricked up," Sinclair explained. "We couldn't get into it without tearing it all down. And do you know what I think, Grandy? I think it would be wiser to take away the chimney-piece up here, and do our investigating from this end. Then, if we find anything, it will all be in this room, and not in the cellar, where the servants can pry about."

"I quite agree with you," said Mrs. Cromarty, "and I put the whole matter in your hands. You and Robert are the sons of the house, and it is your right to manage its affairs."

"Then I say, tear it down at once," cried Bob. "We needn't damage the carving itself, and all that we break away of plaster or inner woodwork can easily be repaired, whatever our success may be."

"Shall we begin now?" asked Sinclair, doubtfully. He was not so impetuous as Bob, and would have been quite willing to study over the matter first.

"Yes, indeed!" cried his impatient brother. "I'm not going to waste a minute. I'm glad I'm a bit of a carpenter. Though not an expert, I can tear down if I can't build up."

"But we must take it down carefully," said Sinclair. "These screws must come out first." But Bob had already gone for tools, and soon returned with screw-drivers, chisels, gimlets, and all the paraphernalia of a carpenter's well-appointed tool-chest.

"Here goes!" he cried, as he put the big screw-driver in the first screw. "Good luck to the Cromartys and three cheers for Uncle Marmaduke and Patty Fairfield!"

CHAPTER XIX

THE DISCOVERY

THE removal of the old chimney-piece was not an easy task. If the Hartley boys hadn't been big and strongly-built, they could scarcely have succeeded in tearing away the woodwork from the wall. But they did do it, and their labours were rewarded by the discovery of the long-lost fortune!

Sure enough the historic " poke " was a pocket or recess between the old bedhead and the main wall. It was really built in the chimney itself, though not in the flue. But this chimney-place, with its wonderfully carved mantel, was never used for fires, and the fortune had remained undisturbed in its hiding-place.

As the boys lifted away the portion of the heavy oak that covered the secret pocket, a rough wall of plaster was seen, and by tapping on it, Sinclair learned that it was hollow.

" Shall we break through? " he said. " I feel sure the money is there."

" Break through, of course," cried Bob; " but

wait a moment till I lock the doors. This is no time for intruders."

Bob fastened the doors, and then with a hatchet they broke through the plaster.

And even as the old mortar crumbled beneath their blows, out fell a shower of glittering gold coins and tightly folded banknotes!

The sight was too much for the strained nerves of the watchers. Mabel burst into tears, and Mrs. Cromarty trembled like a leaf.

The boys broke into shouts of joy, and Patty scarcely knew whether to laugh or cry. But in a moment they were all congratulating each other and showering praises on Patty for her cleverness in the matter.

"It's ours! It's ours!" cried Bob. "It's Grandy's, to be sure, but it belongs to old Cromarty Manor, and we're all Cromartys. Patty, you're hereby adopted and made one of us."

"What shall we do with it?" asked the more practical Sinclair. "I mean, just at present. We must take care of it, at once, you know. We can't leave it long like this."

"There's the old Spanish chest," said Mrs. Hartley, indicating a good-sized affair that stood nearby. "Put it in that."

The Discovery

"Just the thing," said Bob. "Lend a hand, Clair."

It was a strange proceeding. The old coins, many of them still bright, though of far back dates, represented a great deal of money. How much, they could not guess as yet, but it was surely a large sum. Also there were Bank of England notes, folded small that they might be pushed through the openings in the carved oak, and well-preserved, as the pocket had been carefully made damp-proof.

The boys took the money out in double handfuls and deposited it in the old Spanish chest.

"It will be quite safe there until to-morrow," said Mrs. Hartley, "and then we must get it to the bank. But as no one yet knows of our discovery, there can be no danger of its being stolen to-night."

"What ever made Uncle Marmaduke choose this way of concealing his fortune?" asked Bob, as he kept on transferring the money from its hiding-place to the chest.

"He had a fear of banks or investments," said Mrs. Cromarty. "I've often heard him say he wouldn't trust any of them. He said he'd rather be sure of his principal, and go without his interest."

"Crickets!" said Bob, "if all this *had* been out at interest for forty years, think how it would have increased!"

"Yes," said his mother, "but in that case it would not have been hidden, and before now. it might have all been spent."

"Then I'm glad the old gentleman chose this way of banking. And I suppose he meant to leave full instructions where to find it."

"Well," said Sinclair, "we found it without his instructions, thanks to our Patty."

And then they all began again to bless and praise Patty, until she was really embarrassed at their overwhelming gratitude.

"We'd offer you a share," said Bob, gaily, "but you already have more than you know what to do with."

"Perhaps not quite that," said Patty, smiling, "but I have enough. And, oh! I am *so* glad that you have your own at last."

"How much do you suppose there is?" asked Mabel, awe-struck, as she watched the boys still carrying their precious handfuls across the room.

"Enough to buy you some new frocks, sister," said Sinclair, "and enough to fix up dear old Cromarty as it should be fixed up."

The Discovery

"There must be thousands of pounds," said Grandma Cromarty. "To think of Marmaduke exchanging all his securities and bonds for gold and notes! I suppose he did it while I was away in London. He was a most erratic man."

"Well, you see," said Sinclair, thoughtfully, "once he had the place built, he could drop his money through whenever he received any. I can imagine the old chap, after every one else in the house was in bed, standing here and dropping in his coins one by one, and listening to them clink. Why, it's like a child's toy savings-bank, on a large scale."

"It's a large scale!" said Bob. "Whew! I'm tired out. But it's nearly all in the chest now, and see, Grandy, the chest is nearly full! When shall we count it? And how *shall* we get this mess cleared away? If the servants come in here, they'll know it all, at once. And I think we ought to keep the matter quiet until we can cart the gold away to the bank."

"I think so too," said his mother. "Suppose we leave this room exactly as it is, and lock it all up until to-morrow. Then we can talk it over this evening, and decide what is best to do.

I think we should consult with Lawyer Ashton, and let him advise us."

So, after carefully securing the windows, and locking all the doors of the room, it was a merry-hearted family who went away to dress for dinner.

" Let's put on our prettiest frocks, and make the dinner a sort of celebration feast," said Patty, who dearly loved an " occasion."

" We will," said Mabel, " and Grandy must wear her black velvet."

Mrs. Cromarty was easily persuaded, and the happy old lady looked almost regal as, in her trailing gown, she led the way to the dining-room. The dinner conversation was on the all-absorbing topic, and Patty realised afresh how dearly these people loved their old home, and how anxious they were to devote their newly-found fortune to restoring the glories of the place.

" And now we can have the garden party!" exclaimed Mabel. " You know, Patty, we've had one every summer for years and years, and this summer we thought we couldn't afford it. What fun to have you here to it!"

" Let's have it soon," said Sinclair. " Can you get ready in a week, mother?"

The Discovery

"Give me a little longer than that, son. And we want to send out the invitations about ten days before the party."

"We'll make the lists to-night. Let's invite everybody. I suppose, after we put the money safely away, there's no necessity for secrecy about it."

"No, I think not. All our friends will rejoice with us, that we've found it at last."

Later on, they all sat round the library table, and made plans for the garden party. Patty discovered that it would be a much larger and more important affair than she had imagined. The invitation list soon rose to about four hundred, and seemed literally to include everybody in all the country round.

"I really ought to have a new frock for the party," said Mabel; "but we've so much going on that I won't have time to get one made."

This gave Patty an idea, and she determined to give Mabel a little surprise. While they were making the plans for the fête, she was planning to write to Lady Hamilton and ask her to send down from London two new frocks for herself and Mabel to wear at the garden party. She felt sure she could secretly procure one of Mabel's old dresses to send for a pattern, and she meant that Mabel should not know of it until the new frock arrived.

The evening was a merry one, indeed. The boys were so exuberant that they laughed and sang snatches of songs, and exclaimed over and over how much they appreciated the good turn Patty had done them.

The two elder ladies were more quietly glad, and it did Patty's heart good to see that the sad, anxious expression was gone from Mabel's face.

The days before the garden party flew by quickly, for there was much to be done. Extra servants had to be secured, some repairing done in house and gardens, and the caterer's orders attended to. The day before the party the dresses arrived from London. Lady Hamilton had chosen them, though Patty had given her a general idea of what she wanted.

Though they were called white muslin frocks, they were made almost entirely of fine embroidery and lace. Mabel's was worn over a pink silk slip, and Patty's over blue. Frenchy knots of ribbon were placed here and there, and when the boxes were opened and the tissue papers torn away, Mabel gave a shriek of delight at the beautiful things.

The Discovery

Patty had wanted to give Mabel a pretty frock, but had hesitated to do so, lest she wound her pride.

But this seemed different, and Patty offered the gift so prettily, as a souvenir of the garden party, that Mabel accepted it in the spirit it was given.

The day of the party was perfect. Just the right temperature, and not a cloud in the blue sky, except some fleecy little white ones that were as innocent as kittens.

The party was from three till six, and promptly at three o'clock the guests began to arrive. There was a continuous stream of carriages and motor cars, and soon Patty was almost bewildered by the crowds of people. Although introduced to them as they arrived, she couldn't remember them all. But many of them she had met before, and after a time she and Mabel were excused from the receiving party, and were sent to mingle with the guests.

The old place was looking its best. Though there had not been time for much work on the gardens, yet a deal of tidying up had been done. New flowers had been set out in the formal flower beds, the fountains had been repaired and put in working order, and the shrubs and hedges had been trimmed. Patty, looking very sweet in her lovely white dress, wandered around indoors and out, greeting old friends and making new ones.

The house was thrown open, and of course the old chimney-piece, which had been replaced, was scrutinised with great interest. Patty was lionised until she became almost embarrassed at being made so prominent. But everybody was thoroughly glad that the Cromartys had come into their fortune at last. On the lawn was a band of musicians in gay scarlet and gold uniforms, who played popular music at intervals during the afternoon. The terraces and gardens were filled with groups of people pleasantly chatting, and the ladies' pretty summer costumes added to the brilliancy of the scene.

At four o'clock tea was served in a great round tent, which had been put up for the purpose. Although called tea, the repast was a substantial supper of various and elaborate viands. Patty thought she had never seen so many sorts of salads and carefully constructed cold dishes. She sat at a small table with the Merediths and some other young people.

" You're going to stay here all summer, aren't

you?" asked Tom, who sincerely hoped she was.

"I don't know," replied Patty. "I'd love to stay, for I'm happy every minute here. But my own people are writing me very urgently to join them in Switzerland. They're in such delightful quarters there, that they think I'd like it too."

"Oh, don't go. Stay here with us. We're going to get up a croquet club, and we want you to be a member."

"I'll be glad to, if I stay. But where are the people going now?"

The guests had all risen, and were being led to a part of the grounds where a platform had been erected. On this were a troupe of entertainers called The Pierrots. They all wore funny white suits, with little black pompons bobbing all over them. They sang amusing songs, played on cymbals and other instruments, did some clever acrobatic work, and for a half-hour entertained the guests who stood about on the grass, or sat on camp chairs to watch them.

At six o'clock the guests all took leave, and the great procession of vehicles again appeared on the driveway. Mrs. Cromarty and Mrs. Hartley received their good-byes, and Patty and

Patty's Friends

Mabel invited a number of the young people to remain to dine and spend the evening.

"Though I'm sure we can't eat any dinner, after that very satisfying tea," said Grace Meredith, as she accepted the invitation.

In the evening they all went out on the lake for a moonlight row. Several new boats had been bought, and the young men rowed the girls about. The boats were hung with Chinese lanterns, which gave the lake the appearance of a regatta or a water festival.

Then back to the house for a dance in the great hall . The musicians had remained, and to their inspiriting strains the young people glided about in merry measures.

"Do give me another waltz," Tom Meredith begged of Patty.

"I'd be glad to, Tom," said Patty, frankly; "but I can't do it without offending somebody else. I love to dance with you, but you've had three already, and I've promised all the rest."

But Tom wheedled Mrs. Hartley into allowing one more extra, after the last dance, and he claimed Patty for that.

"You're the best dancer I ever saw," said Tom, as they floated away.

"You're the best English dancer I ever saw,"

laughed Patty, for she well knew English people do not dance like Americans. Good-natured Tom didn't mind her implication, and after the waltz was ended he led her out on the terrace to sit down for a bit and rest. There were several others there, the Hartley boys among them, and soon they began to sing songs.

Others came and joined them, and the young voices rose in merry choruses and glees.

"You have splendid songs in England," said Patty, after the men's voices had come out strong in "Hearts of Oak" and "Rule Britannia."

"Yes, we have," agreed Tom. "But, Patty, won't you sing something alone?"

"Do," chorused the rest, and Mabel said: "Sing that newest song that you and Sinclair made."

"'The Moon's Song?'" asked Patty.

"Yes; this is just the night for it."

The moon was nearing the western horizon, and its soft light fell across the lake in silver ripples. Truly it was just the time and place to sing the pretty song of which Patty had composed the words, and Sinclair had set them to music. It was a simple air, but full of soft, lingering cadences, and without accompaniment

[267]

Patty's Friends

Patty's really sweet voice sounded exquisite as it thrilled through the summer evening air.

The song was called "The Minstrel Moon," and the words were these:

"I wonder if the moon could sing,
  On a marvellous, mystical night in spring,
  I wonder what the song would be
  That the minstrel moon would sing to me.
  And as I think, I seem to know
  How the music of the moon would go.
  It would be a mystic, murmuring strain
  Like the falling of far-away fairy rain.
  Just a soft and silvery song
  That would swing and swirl along;
      Not a word
      Could be heard
  But a lingering ding-a-dong.
  Just a melody low and sweet,
  Just a harmony faint and fleet,
      Just a croon
      Of a tune
  Is the Music of the Moon."

CHAPTER XX

ONE beautiful morning, about a week after the garden party, Patty lay in her favourite hammock out under the trees.

She liked this hammock especially, for from it she could see both terraces, the formal gardens, and the lake beyond.

As she looked around this morning she could see the workmen busily engaged in restoring the gardens to their original symmetry and beauty. The Hartleys were by no means purse proud or ostentatious, and their sudden acquisition of a great fortune in no way changed their simple, pleasant attitude toward life. But they were now enabled to live in their dear old home, without financial anxieties, and moreover, were able to repair and restore its appointments.

But though Patty loved to let her idle gaze roam over the attractive landscape, her thoughts just now were far away. She had in her hand a letter from her father, and its message was

[269]

strongly in favour of her leaving Cromarty Manor and joining her parents in Switzerland. It was for Patty to make choice, but both Nan and Mr. Fairfield urged the plan they proposed. So Patty was thinking it over. She was very happy at Cromarty, and the life was quiet and pleasant, and interspersed with many little gaieties. But she thought, herself, it was a pity not to travel about and see sights and places when opportunity presented itself.

As she lay, thinking, she saw a large motor-car coming along the drive through the park. She jumped out of the hammock and started toward the house, in order to greet the guests whoever they might be. As the car came nearer, she saw a lady and gentleman in the tonneau, but so concealed were they by their motor-clothes she could not recognise them.

As they drew nearer, the lady waved her hand, and seeing the familiar gesture, Patty at once realised that it was Lady Hamilton.

Her father was with her, and Patty ran to meet them, and reached the steps of the great entrance of Cromarty just as the car swung round the last curve of the road.

"Oh, Kitty!" cried Patty; "I'm *so* glad to see you! Where did you come from? Why

Good-byes

didn't you tell me you were coming? How do you do, Sir Otho. This is indeed a surprise."

"How are you, my dear child?" said Sir Otho Markleham, after Patty had released Lady Kitty from her enthusiastic embrace, and turned to shake hands with her father.

"Come in," said Patty, dancing about in her excited glee. "Come right in. You are welcome to Cromarty Manor, and in a moment the family will also tell you so."

"What a delightful house!" said Lady Hamilton, pausing to admire the stately old portal.

"Yes, isn't it? You know the Hartleys, don't you?"

"Slightly. I'll be glad to see them again. But, of course, we came to see you."

"And it's a lovely surprise. Are you staying near here?"

"Only for a day or two," said Sir Otho. "We're taking a little jaunt about, and as Kitty wanted to see you especially, we came in this direction."

The chauffeur and the big touring car were put in charge of the Cromarty coachman, and Patty ushered her guests into the house.

The ladies soon appeared and with hospitable

[271]

welcome insisted that Sir Otho and his daughter should remain for a few days. This they were unable to do, but it was finally decided that they should stay the night, and resume their trip the next day.

"And," said Sir Otho, "it may seem a rather sudden proceeding, but we want to take Patty with us."

"Take Patty!" exclaimed Mabel, aghast; "for how long?"

"You tell her," said Sir Otho, smiling at his daughter. "I haven't the courage."

"I'll explain later," said Lady Hamilton. "But now, I want to enjoy the beauties of this grand old place. Is this the celebrated apartment where the fortune was hidden?"

"Yes," said Patty, who had written to Lady Kitty about the matter. "And here is the old chimney-piece."

"You can imagine, Lady Hamilton," said Mrs. Hartley, "the deep debt of gratitude we are under to our dear Patty."

"You must be, indeed. But I know Patty is quite as glad that she made the discovery as you are yourselves."

The rest of the morning was devoted to showing the visitors about the place. Sir Otho was greatly interested in the plans for the restoration of the gardens, and both he and Lady Kitty were enraptured with the historic treasures of the old house. After luncheon, Lady Hamilton unfolded her plans to Patty.

"I have been in correspondence with Mr. and Mrs. Fairfield," she said, "and we've concluded that we must have Patty back with us again. She has been very happy here, I know, but she has made you a long visit, and I've really been sent down here to kidnap her."

Patty smiled, but the others didn't. Mrs. Cromarty and Mrs. Hartley looked truly sorry, and Mabel had to struggle to keep her tears back.

"You are right," said Mrs. Cromarty, at last. "We have enjoyed having Patty here more than I can tell you. But we must not be selfish. I know her parents have been writing for her to go to them, and it is wrong for us to urge her to stay here."

"But I don't want Patty to go away," said Mabel, and now she was really crying.

"I know you don't, dearie," said her mother. "But I see it as Grandma does, and I think we must let her go. Perhaps some time she'll come again."

Patty's Friends

Patty's Friends

" Oh, I hope so," said Patty, smiling through
the tears that had gathered in her own eyes.
" You've all been so good to me, and I've had
such lovely times."

The question once settled, Lady Hamilton
went on to say that she proposed to take
Patty away the next day. Of course this
redoubled Mabel's woe, but Lady Kitty was
firm.

" It would be just as hard to spare her a week
hence," she said. " And then, who would take
her to London? If she goes with us to-morrow,
we will keep her with us for the rest of our
motor tour—about a week—and then reach
London about the first of July. After that
Patty and I will join Mr. and Mrs. Fairfield
in Switzerland, and go on to do some further
travelling."

Although Patty was sorry to leave Cromarty,
this plan did sound delightful, and she was glad
that it was all settled for her, and she had no
further responsibility in the matter.

Lady Hamilton had a genius for despatch, and
she superintended the packing of Patty's clothes
and belongings that same afternoon. Except
for the luggage needed on the motor-tour, everything was to be sent to Lady Kitty's home in

London, and Patty had to smile, as she realised that her present temporary home was the great house where she had so daringly braved the irascible Sir Otho.

There was a daintily furnished room in the Markleham house that had been set aside for Patty's very own, and whenever she cared to she was invited to occupy it.

When the boys came home that afternoon and heard the news, they set up a wail of woe that was both genuine and very noisy.

No one could help admiring Lady Kitty, but Sinclair and Bob felt as if she were robbing their household, and it required all their good manners to hide their feeling of resentment.

But they rose nobly to the occasion, and Bob said: " Well, since Patty must go, we'll have to send her off in a blaze of glory. Let's make a party, mother, a few people to dinner, and some more for the evening."

Mrs. Hartley quickly realised that this would be the best way to tide over a sad occasion, and she agreed. The Merediths and a few others were sent for to come to dinner, and a dozen or more young people asked for a little dance in the evening. Notwithstanding her unwelcome errand, Lady Kitty fitted right into the house party, and both she and her father were so affable and pleasant that the Hartleys forgave them for stealing Patty away.

The tourists had luggage with them, so were able to don attire suitable to the party. Lady Hamilton wore one of her beautiful trailing lace gowns, which had won for her Patty's name of "The White Lady."

Patty, too, wore a white frock, of ruffled organdie, with touches of pale green velvet. In her pretty hair was a single pink rose, and as she arranged it, she felt a pang as she thought that might be the last flower she would ever wear from the dear old Cromarty rose garden. The dinner was a beautiful feast, indeed. The table sparkled with the old silver and glass that had belonged to the Cromarty ancestors. Flowers were everywhere, and the table and dining-room were lighted entirely by wax candles, with the intent of abiding by the old traditions of the manor.

At Patty's plate was a multitude of gifts. How they managed it on such short notice, she never knew, but every one of the family and most of the guests gave her a parting souvenir.

Grandma Cromarty gave her a valuable old

miniature that had long been in her historic collection. Mrs. Hartley gave her an exquisite
fan, painted by a celebrated artist. Mabel gave
her a ring set with a beautiful pearl, and the
boys together gave her a splendid set of
Dickens' works in elaborately gilded binding.
Grace Meredith brought her a bangle, and
Tom a quaint old-fashioned candlestick; and
many other guests brought pretty or curious
trifles.

Patty was overwhelmed at this unexpected
kindness, and opened parcel after parcel in a
bewilderment of delight.

Everybody was gay and merry, yet there was
an undercurrent of sadness, as one after another
remembered this was the last time they would
see pretty Patty.

After dinner they all assembled on the terrace,
and the other guests, arriving later, joined them
there.

But the soft beauty of the summer evening
seemed to intensify the spirit of sadness, and
all were glad to hear the strains of a violin
coming from the great hall.

Bob had sent for two or three musicians, and
soon the young people were spinning around in
the dance, and merriment once more reigned.

Patty's Friends

Always a popular partner, Patty was fairly besieged that night.

"I can't," she said laughingly, as the young men gathered around to beg her favours; "I've halved every dance already; I can't do more than that."

"Don't halve this one," said Tom Meredith, as he led her away for a waltz. "I must have all of it. Unless you'll sit it out with me on the terrace."

"No, thank you," said Patty. "I'd rather dance. I don't suppose I'll find another dancer as good as you all summer."

"I hate to think of your going away," said Tom. "You almost promised me you'd stay here all summer."

"I know. But I'm not mistress of my own plans. They're made for me."

"And you're glad of it," said Tom, almost angrily. "You're glad you're going away from here—to go motoring in Switzerland, and all sorts of things."

"Don't be so savage. It isn't surprising that I'm glad to go away from any one as cross as you are."

Tom had to smile in return for Patty's laughing tones, and he said more gently:

Good-byes

"I don't mean to be bearish, but I wish you weren't going. I—I like you an awful lot, Patty. Truly I do."

"I'm glad of it," said Patty, heartily, "and I like you too. After Sinclair and Bob, you're the nicest boy in England."

"There's luck in odd numbers," said Tom, a little ruefully, "so I'm glad I'm number three. But I'd like to be number one."

"Well, you're a number one dancer," said Patty, as the music ceased, and with that Tom had to be content.

And now the hour was getting late and the young people began to go home.

It was really an ordeal for Patty to say good-bye, for she had many friends among them, and they all seemed truly regretful to part with her.

But after they had gone, and only those staying in the house remained, another surprise was in waiting for Patty. They were gathered in the great hall, talking over for the last time the mystery of the hidden fortune, and Patty's clever solution of it.

"And now," said Sinclair, "I've a little speech to make."

He went and stood on the "stair across the

hall," in front of the old chimney-piece, and so, just beneath the picture of the fir trees. The painting was a fine one, and represented a landscape with firs in the foreground. It had hung there since the days of the earlier Cromartys, and was a valuable work of art.

Patty had always loved the picture, even before the added interest of learning the truth about the fir trees, and they all knew it was one of her favourites among the many art treasures of the old house.

"I was going to make this speech when the party was here," proceeded Sinclair, "but I didn't, partly because I feared it might embarrass Patty, and partly because I like it better to have only our own people here. But the speech itself is this: We, the Cromartys of Cromarty Manor, realising that we can never liquidate the great debt of gratitude we owe to our beautiful and beloved friend, Miss Patty Fairfield, wish, at least, to give her a token of our affection and a memento of her noble deed. We, therefore, one and all of the household of Cromarty, offer her this picture of fir trees, this painting by Hobbema, and we trust that she will accept it in the spirit it is tendered."

[280]

Good-byes

Sinclair bowed and sat down, and Patty sat for a moment in awestruck silence.

Then, "The Hobbema!" she cried, "I won't take it! The idea of giving me that painting! Why, it's one of the gems of the house!"

"That's why we want you to have it, Patty dear," said Grandma Cromarty, gently. "It is one of our treasures, and for that very reason it is worthy to be presented as a souvenir to one who so gloriously deserves it."

"Hear! Hear!" cried Bob. "Grandy makes a better speech than you, Clair."

Patty's scruples were lovingly overcome, and she was made to realise that she was the owner of a real masterpiece of art, that would be to her a lifelong delight.

"But what will take its place?" she said. "It has hung there so many years."

"It hung there," said Mrs. Hartley, "until its mission was fulfilled. Now that there is nothing to be searched for ' between the fir trees and the oak,' it need hang there no longer. It is fitting that we retain the ' oak ' and you possess the ' fir trees,' thus assuring an everlasting bond of union between the fir trees and the oak."

"Bravo, Mater!" cried Bob. "You're coming out strong on speechifying, too. Mabel, we must look out for our laurels."

But Mabel was too near the verge of tears to trust her voice, so she slipped her hand in Patty's, knowing that she would understand all that could not be said.

"Well," went on Bob, "I'm not much of an orator, but I'll take it for my part to see that the Fir Trees are properly packed and sent to your home, Patty. Where shall I send the box?"

"I hate to have it go to New York now," said Patty, "for I want it with me while I'm over here."

So it was arranged to send the picture to Sir Otho's house in London, there to remain until the Fairfields returned to America.

The departure from Cromarty was made next morning directly after breakfast. It was fortunate that the last details of luggage preparations, and the packing of luncheon and so forth, made a bustle and hurry that left little time for actual farewells. And, too, they were all too sensible to mar Patty's last memory of Cromarty with futile regrets.

So after good-byes were said, and the party

stowed away in the big car, Sinclair started one of their favourite nonsense songs.

The others joined in, and Patty sang too, and handkerchiefs were waved, and as the car slid out of sight among the trees, those who were left could still hear Patty's high, sweet soprano ringing back to them.